PROFITS
UNLIMITED

PROFITS
UNLIMITED

A Wall Street Insider Reveals the
Secret to Life-Changing Wealth

PAUL MAMPILLY

BANYAN HILL

Banyan Hill Publishing
P.O. Box 8378
Delray Beach, FL 33482
Tel.: 866-584-4096
Email: http://banyanhill.com/contact-us
Web: http://banyanhill.com

ISBN: 978-0-578-57688-6

Notice: this publication is designed to provide accurate and authoritative information in regard to the subject matter covered. It is sold and distributed with the understanding that the authors, publisher and seller are not engaged in rendering legal, accounting or other professional advice or services. If legal or other expert assistance is required, the services of a competent professional adviser should be sought.

The information and recommendations contained in this book have been compiled from sources considered reliable. Employees, officers and directors of Banyan Hill do not receive fees or commissions for any recommendations of services or products in this publication. Investment and other recommendations carry inherent risks. As no investment recommendation can be guaranteed, Banyan Hill takes no responsibility for any loss or inconvenience if one chooses to accept them.

Banyan Hill advocates full compliance with applicable tax and financial reporting laws. U.S. law requires income taxes to be paid on all worldwide income wherever a U.S. person (citizen or resident alien) may live or have a residence. Each U.S. person who has a financial interest in, or signature authority over bank, securities, or other financial accounts in a foreign country that exceeds $10,000 in aggregate value, must report that fact on his or her federal income tax return, IRS form 1040. An additional report must be filed by April 15th of each year on an information return (FinCEN form 114) with the U.S. Treasury. IRS form 8938 also may be due on April 15th annually, depending on the total value of foreign assets. Willful noncompliance may result in criminal prosecution. You should consult a qualified attorney or accountant to ensure that you know, understand and comply with these and any other reporting requirements.

DEDICATION

I dedicate this to my family, my family at work at Banyan Hill and my beloved subscribers and readers.

ACKNOWLEDGEMENTS

Many strong hands assisted in the development of "Profits Unlimited: A Wall Street Insider Reveals the Secret to Life-Changing Wealth." Without their efforts, this book wouldn't have been published.

My sincere appreciation goes to Jaclyn Frakes-Jones, my managing editor, for her time and meticulous editing skills to ensure we published a book we are all proud and excited to share with readers.

To Sarah Glassman, my publisher, Nick Tate, my senior editorial manager, and Tamara Barkhanoy, my investment research analyst, for all their input and insights.

To Jennifer Somerville for overseeing the development of the book.

To Alexandra Dreibelbis and her entire proofing team for making sure each word is properly written.

And to Mary Branch and Liam Sanelli for their graphic design expertise.

What subscribers to PROFITS UNLIMITED are saying about Paul Mampilly:

"Thank you for giving us here in mainstream America the golden opportunity and inestimable chance to achieve the 'American Dream.' You are truly the greatest of catalysts to make our highest hopes and dreams come true. Thanks again for this priceless opportunity." — Tim R.

"My husband says it's like somebody else is in this house making another income for us — Paul Mampilly! So that's really great." — Michael K.

"In 10 days, our account value went up by $627,573.16." — Gretta C.

"There is just this happy, happy feeling, and we're just very excited and consider him not only our financial advisor, but our coach." — Charles L.

"I'm up well over $100,000. Thank you, Paul!!" — Matt A.

"My $36,500 investment sits now at $57,600." — Jeff M.

"There's no hype in Paul. He's straight, honest, down-to-earth and gives it to you the way it is." — Ian S.

"I have made $65,000 in profit." — John D.

"One of the things I really like about the service is that Paul, in particular, is an optimist. And it really shines through." — Warren H.

"I have made over $10,000 the past couple months and [I'm] having a blast." — Mark R.

"If it weren't for your expertise and guidance, the regular folk, like me, would have no chance whatsoever in making some significant money in the stock market." — Stanley V.

"Since October 1, my portfolio is up $167,000." — Sam L.

"WOW! In just over two weeks [I've made] $12,000 in gains." — Nicholas B.

"Thank you for sharing your insight and expertise with the regular folk and giving us the opportunity to make some supplemental income in such a user-friendly way." — Susan K.

"When I started, we had $175,000 in cash. Today, our cash balance is over $900,000." — Aaron C.

"You are like my investing guru, but a friend as well." — Sandra P.

"We made over $10,000 in just a month." — Jay E.

"So far, I have made $150,000." — Charles P.

"He's very down to earth. He wants to help people make money. Obviously he can do this for people with billions and just have to deal with a few folks, but he's got a great heart just trying to help others build their wealth. And I really appreciate what he's doing." — Kenneth W.

"My E-Trade account [went] from $88,000 to $159,000." — Michael R.

"This one stock paid for my lifetime membership. I respect your experience and love the [service]." — Joel F.

"Up 125%, over $7,000 in gains." — Gina O.

"The money I made went a long way in helping to pay for my wedding. Keep up the good work; you're making a real difference in people's lives." — Elliot F.

"My portfolio just soared $10,000." — Kim S.

"Paul Mampilly provides clarity. He is a breath of fresh air in a very unclear, convoluted marketplace. He is focused, he is uplifting." — Phil S.

"I am up about $12,000." — Steve L.

"I really liked your 'millennial-driven growth' concept … I bought some [stock] after reading your report and the stock is up more than 150%. Thank you!"
— Larry C.

TABLE OF CONTENTS

Letter to You, From a Fellow Reader 1

Part 1: A Young Man's Passage From India 5

Making Money for Rich People, a Wall Street Reality 12

Why Stocks Go Up Most of the Time, but Fall Sometimes 15

Behavior Finance: Unlearning What College Finance
Taught Me 19

My Own Skin in the Game 23

Helping Ordinary Investors Live Comfortably 24

Part 2: How to Capitalize on a Life-Changing Bull
Market 29

What Ordinary Investors Do Wrong That Holds Them Back ... 30

Start off Small, It's the Best Way to Stay Humble 31

Why Stocks Always Win vs. Other Investments 34

Don't Let Fear Trump Facts in Today's Economy 36

The Future Is Now, Once Again 37

Don't Forget the Simple Secret for Picking Great Stocks 40

Part 3: Rules of the Game — The Secrets to Success
in the Stock Market 43

How I Pick Stocks 44

The Heart of Every Explosive Stock Pick 46

How I Knew Netflix Was a Buy 47

Targeting Massive Winners that Will Beat Warren Buffett's
Portfolio 50

Grab Winners on the Way Up — My "GoingUpness" System 52

Inside the "GoingUpness" System 55

InDemandness 57

Insiderness 58

Buyness 58

ScarceAbility 59

ValueAbility 60

ManageAbility 61

Navigate the Markets Like a Pro with These Easy Rules 62

Determining the Right Time to Buy 66

How to Deal With "Market Maker" Manipulation 68

How You Should Sell: Limit Orders vs. Market Orders 69

Why Stocks Can, and Should, Be Volatile 71

7 Things to Know Before You Start Trading 71

Part 4: Building Your Financial Future With the Big Profits Unlimited Mega Trends 79

Mega Trend No. 1: The Internet of Things (IoT) 80

Harness Cloud Computing's Limitless Profit Potential 87

Mega Trend No. 2: Robotics and Artificial Intelligence 90

Rise of the Robots: Tap This Disruptive Technology for Big Gains 93

Mega Trend No. 3: Precision Medicine 95

Profit From the Precision Medicine Mega Trend 100

Mega Trend No. 4: Millennials 108

Mega Trend No. 5: Autonomous Vehicles 114

Mega Trend No. 6: Blockchain 118

Lock in Big Gains From the Blockchain Revolution 123

Mega Trend No. 7: New Energy Technology 128

Spotting the Energy Company Fueling a 700% Gain 136

Part 5: Hold Strong Hands for Success in the Stock Market 149

Appendix 155

Make Explosive Gains in These 2 Markets for "Advanced" Investors 156

Market No. 1: IPOs — Don't Let Fear Stop You From Playing the Game 156

Market No. 2: Options — Navigate the Market Like a Wall Street Investor 160

More From Paul Mampilly — Bold Profits Premium Content 173

LETTER TO YOU, FROM A FELLOW READER

Dear Reader,

My story could be your story. It already may be. What you may learn — or can attest to — from my story is there's something to learn by reading this book. Let me explain...

The depth and breadth of my good fortune resides within a gift that I have been given.

This gift, which gratefully has led me along a special road, is crossing paths with Paul Mampilly. His immense talent and unrelenting character ... his care and "compassion without condition" for those who have come to know him ... has changed my life. It's changed my family's life.

I had been reading financial newsletters for about seven years. I had learned many investing strategies. Even so, I had yet to make any meaningful amount of money.

Then, I found Paul.

It was mid-2016. I watched Paul's first video.

As I watched it and listened to Paul, I was mesmerized.

He brought to life the "Internet of Things." He expressed how it would help breathe intelligence into inanimate objects. To communicate. To collect data. To improve our lives in ways that would push the bounds of imagination.

From that one encounter, Paul taught me about a whole world I didn't understand. He opened my eyes to a concept that few truly understand even today: disruptive technology. And it's why I was so taken to watch Paul's first video over 50 times. I find myself watching all of his videos multiple times because each time, I always learn something new.

As days went by, and the more I studied Paul's financial newsletter *Profits Unlimited*, the more Paul's recommendations, exciting entities and exotic business models all came to life right before me, at light speed.

I read that Paul was a Wall Street legend. My wife, Victoria, noticed a voice with hope in it and a compelling smile.

Much of Paul's life, revealed bit by bit amid his financial writings, is tethered to his life in India. To his beloved mother. To his beloved father's resolve. And to finding his way to America.

In those first days of reading Paul's newsletter, we found that Paul was on a mission to honor his parents by honoring us, his followers.

Fast-forward to today — we continue to thrive, thanks to Paul's commitment to helping his readers, working day and night for our benefit.

As we studied Paul, my wife and I overcame our trepidation and began to invest.

By the end of 2017, we had generated gains of $1,500,000.

"Wow. How could this be!" my wife and I thought. These gains changed our lives. We could hardly believe that the numbers in our brokerage account were actually ours.

Because of Paul, our personal net worth today is beyond anything we ever dreamed. And we believe it is positioned to grow dramatically and explosively in the years to come.

My wife and I continue to follow Paul's recommendations. We continue to learn from his wisdom. We continue to put our trust in him.

Here's what I can say emphatically...

Paul Mampilly is the real deal. He is smart. He speaks from his heart, with sincere integrity. He is not just an investor; he is a teacher. Yes, he has an impressive resume. But even more so, he has a respectable character. He has a legendary and visionary talent.

Following Paul and his recommendations have taught us how to be smart investors. We have learned about Paul's GoingUpness system for identifying investment opportunities. We have learned the importance of starting off small and about equal weight investing. We have learned about the psychology of investing. We have learned so much more.

As an investor, you either do the research yourself or you gain faith in someone else. Our experience and good fortune in trusting in Paul and his system has been a gift for our entire family. We now mentor our adult grandchildren in his one-of-a-kind investment models.

Should you elect to join us, those of us who invest in following Paul's insights, employ this book as your personal manual.

John H Bertrand
Founder and Chairman
JH Bertrand Inc.

PART -1-

A Young Man's Passage From India

My father is my hero.

My dad, Thomas, was born in 1933 in a tiny village in India at a time when the country was incredibly poor, with people dying of hunger every day. My dad's mother died when he was just three years old, and his father passed away when he was 20.

When many people think of India, they think of Gandhi or maybe Mother Teresa. Perhaps, if they know a bit more about the country, they think of Dominique Lapierre's 1985 bestseller "City of Joy" or Gregory David Roberts' novel "Shantaram." Maybe even the Oscar-winning movie "Slumdog Millionaire."

Many are becoming increasingly familiar with the economic success stories of India too — the call centers, manufacturing boom and the country's growing profile as a modern, large and surprisingly democratic "emerging economy" in the world.

But for now, forget all that. Back in the 1970s, India had less than nothing. And my father even less. Somehow though, he managed to put himself through college. But even when dad got a job in Bombay — India's biggest city, today called Mumbai — he was still broke with a family to support.

Dad was a striver — he knew a few things about risk and reward. In 1974, he applied for a job in Dubai, in the United Arab Emirates, a little-known place at the time. Today, obviously, Dubai is very well-known — a glamorous place full of seven-star hotels and the world's tallest building, the 163-floor Burj Khalifa. But back then nobody had heard of it.

My mother, Susy, tells the story about how everybody told him not to go. They told him: "Don't be a fool," and my mother still remembers his response.

"I have nothing to lose," he said.

I was just five at the time. My dad answered a tiny ad in an Indian newspaper. They were looking for people to move to this completely unknown place. It was all risk, but there was also a huge potential reward for a poor Indian trying to make his way in the world for my mother, sister and me.

Dubai was literally a desert. I still remember my early trips there. I had my first passport — I was too young to be able to sign it, so I had my thumbprint on it instead.

Dad would tell these stories of how he would sit down with the sheikh of Dubai. They're tribal people, the kind of people who today rule places such as Saudi Arabia and the United Arab Emirates. They would sit in this great big fancy tent and drink tiny cups of coffee. They would discuss how to build the electric infrastructure in Dubai. That's how my dad became the equivalent of the chief financial officer of an electric company there.

Dubai, at the time, had just discovered oil. The standard of living and the amount of money my dad was paid was way more than he could ever hope to make. The city grew spectacularly, and Dad made 100,000 times more money than if he'd stayed in India

Clearly, going to Dubai was a no-brainer. By the time he died in 2000, he'd put my sister and me through college. And he'd saved enough so my mom never had to work or worry about money again.

None of that was obvious to us then. "Don't go!" his siblings told him when he got the position. Yet he knew Dubai was a better bet — a calculated risk. It paid off in spades.

When I think about that story, I feel a strong kinship with my father. At the moments that matter now, that's exactly the way I look at things: I have nothing to lose and everything to gain.

Now I see that he's the reason I became an investor. And that his no-lose mentality is why I have been so successful. I take calculated risks and when the payoff is big enough, I get in big. I'll tell you more about this in the chapters ahead.

Because of my dad, I also inherited a love of speculation … investing with the hope of a gain, but also a risk of loss. My mother tells stories of how, when he was young, he was very frustrated at how little money he made.

So sometimes, back then, he would head out to the horse track and make big bets in the hopes of making it big. It made my mom crazy, because they didn't make a lot of money to begin with. Yet she stuck with him.

When you're poor and young in India, you just borrow a tiny amount, usually from a neighbor or relative, to manage the household. If there wasn't money to buy food, you might borrow a few dollars from someone in your apartment building who would lend you the money. Then pay it back as soon as you could. You make do. My mother would run our household this way as needed, but my father liked to speculate.

His passion for speculating eventually led him to the stock market. When he had enough extra money in Dubai, I remember him getting involved in the Indian stock market. He made a tiny amount of money at first, but then the stock market fell apart. He didn't really spend enough time to truly focus on it to be able to make money. He was working hard to support us, and the research you had to do to invest was difficult even for professional investors in India at that time. It's far easier today, for sure.

Besides taking a chance on Dubai, my dad then made one of the best investments ever — one that still pays off.

In the 1980s, India experienced a credit crisis. Essentially, the country ran out of money. The government could not pay its bills. Like every country, it had to have dollars to buy oil, grain and all the commodities denominated in dollars.

So India put out this urgent call for help. The money in Dubai was readily converted to dollars. There were a lot of Indians by then living in Dubai and places like it, such as Qatar and Saudi Arabia. So the government in New Delhi offered Indians abroad three or four times the market rate of interest.

It allowed them to keep the money in dollars if they lent it to India. The interest rate was something between 18% to 22%.

Think about that. A rate of return you might expect from the total U.S. stock market might be 7%, conservatively invested. At that rate, your money doubles in about 10 years. At three times that rate, it doubles in one-third the time! If you put in $100, it became $200 in three years. Then it became $400 three years later, then $800 just like that. In less than a decade, you had almost eight times your initial investment!

Dad saw the brass ring dipping down at last. I remember him taking virtually everything we had and putting it into this scheme offered by the Indian government. We went through some years where every dollar we earned was watched very carefully. We didn't spend money on clothes or shoes. It was very, very tight.

But the bet paid off. I mean, just imagine the compounding. I don't know exactly what he put in, but it might have been $100,000 at 22% for 15 years — enough to turn that considerable sum at the time into almost $2 million. That was an enormous risk he took, but it paid off. My family is still collecting the last of the money from that time.

As a result of those experiences, I became interested in money. I was also widely read, even from the time I was a kid. My father used to subscribe to *Time* magazine, and I remember taking it off his bedside table and reading it. I read about companies such as Apple and the new biotechnology companies. I didn't understand what these things were, but I was interested in them.

In Dubai, at the time, there were virtually no schools — no infrastructure of any sort — so my dad sent my sister and me to a boarding school in India. I was in boarding schools from the time I was about seven until I was about 16.

These were Catholic boarding schools. Most people grow up with their parents, but I grew up by myself. At a young age, I was taking planes and trains by myself, and doing stuff that in today's society might seem unthinkable. Recently, I took my kids to India during their school winter break. While on the plane with them, I said: "You know, just imagine being on the plane by yourself."

They were like: "Yeah, it seems kind of weird, Dad."

That said, one thing I did get out of boarding school was this enormous sense of independence and decision-making from a very early age.

Reading, too, was a big part of building my own identity. I remember very early on, like 11 or 12, reading a textbook which had a description of the Great Depression. The stories stuck in my head, even as a little kid. The affect this thing called the "stock market" had on actual people. I was enamored with how people made money in it. And how it could actually influence a person and his or her entire mental state. This fed my already growing fascination with finance.

So as I mentioned, I left boarding school at the age of 16 and moved back with my parents. I was with them for two years in Dubai. That's when my father started to see that other Indian families were sending their kids to study in the United States, which was kind of a new thing — at the time. We looked into it, and he found that he could afford it. At 18, I ventured out on my own to America.

It was 1986.

I started at Montclair State College in New Jersey. Today it's called Montclair State University. Looking back, it was clearly a different time than what we see today. Now, there are thousands of Indians in the United States: engineers, CEOs and so on. But back then, in the mid-1980s, I was a different face in the crowd.

That said, I was and still am very proud of my upbringing, however meager.

India is on a different planet from the United States, then and now. Coming here as an 18-year-old kid, in hindsight, it was kind of bewildering. I didn't know my head from my foot. It took me a couple years. I wasn't at Harvard or even a mid-level school. I was at that place where the vast majority of the kids were the first generation in their family to go to college.

There was an incredible amount of partying around me, which I didn't really understand or know what to make of it. From my perspective, my father was spending an enormous amount of money to send me here, so I felt an obligation to succeed and to make the best of it. Yet — like many college kids — it took me a couple years to really figure out what to do.

I finally found my bearings by writing for the school newspaper. At that time, Ronald Reagan was recently reelected. And the stock market was flying, which led to some interesting newspaper articles to read and write. Given my continued childhood interest in the stock market, finance just seemed like a very natural subject for me to study.

Eventually, I became an editor on the newspaper and got a degree in finance. I was supposed to graduate in 1990, but got cold feet, thinking: What will I do once I graduate? I panicked at the idea of either having to go back to India or look for a job. So I decided to stay and get a second concentration in accounting. The times weren't any better by the time I graduated in 1991. There was a recession going on, caused by a financial crisis similar to what we had in 2008.

In retrospect, most of college was a complete waste of time. Everything they teach you about finance does not teach you how to make money in the markets. They teach you this very formal view of the industry. I have never used this in my work experience as an investor. Yet, even to this day, unhelpful financial theories still dominate the finance curriculum in college.

In a nutshell, efficient market theory states that stock prices are always right, or nearly enough that it doesn't matter. All the information that you can find on a stock is priced into the stock in real time. So, speculating is pointless. Or so goes the theory. As you will see, nothing could be further from the truth when it comes to real investing.

What did help me? I sought out some internships including one with a financial advisor. She taught me a lot by how she worked. What she did was look at stocks from the "psychological point of view," while also, obviously, doing fundamental work. I learned just how important it is to understand the psychology — how people behave and react — that underpins the marketplace. It is through that experience and what I learned from her that really began my path to where I am today ... in how I observe and evaluate the financial markets.

Making Money for Rich People, a Wall Street Reality

After college, I worked at Bankers Trust. It had a great policy where you could go from one job to another in the company. I posted for a job at the Bankers Trust private bank, where they managed the money of high net worth individuals. I was selected to be an assistant to a portfolio manager.

Eventually, I became a portfolio manager myself. This became my first experience managing money. Here, I decided that I would take my future into my own hands.

Money management businesses for high net worth individuals, at private banks, operated around a very old-fashioned notion of money management. It was very much based on the relationships. The people who managed the actual money weren't particularly skilled technically. They didn't have MBAs, chartered financial analyst (CFA) credentials or anything like that. They were just people who had grown up dealing with old money.

A lot of the clients were widows. You saw accounts where a single stock probably represented 80% of the money in it. I remember seeing lots of wives of executives who had inherited stock in drug companies such as Merck, Bristol-Myers Squibb and Pfizer. Obviously, these executives had gotten stock very early on in their careers, simply held it and it became worth millions of dollars.

Even a simple thing, like diversification (which I'll explain later in this book), wasn't practiced. This is largely because the real job of the people who managed the money was to hold the hand of the client. They'd call them up on their birthdays, remember their kids' birthdays and to write Christmas cards. The money was just kind of left alone.

Then you had this entire new generation of people like me who had an education, at least an academic one, in managing money. People who wanted to implement at least some of it, especially diversification. While I was working at the private bank, I even decided to go back for *more* schooling and get an MBA at Fordham University. I also took the CFA tests to get to that designation, which is still considered one of the hardest to get.

So one of the things I did once I became a portfolio manager was organize the junior people at Bankers Trust into a group. I did this without permission from the authorities or people above me, with the goal to analyze the companies of the stocks we owned in these accounts. We then started to write weekly notes and updates on what these companies were releasing in terms of news and quarterly results. And we started to listen to conference calls and make notes about them. Amazingly, we were resisted. The old guard didn't like it; they thought it threatened them.

Then in 1998, Deutsche Bank, Germany's largest bank, bought Bankers Trust. It converted the private bank to Deutsche and took over all its asset management. Which is how I ended up at Deutsche.

Then, in the middle of 1999, something interesting happened. Some scientists announced that they had sequenced the human genome. I had been assigned to oversee health care.

I quickly became fascinated with this particular sector. Once the human genome breakthrough was announced, these tiny biotech stocks went screaming upward every day ... and we weren't in them!

"You need to go work this out, like right now," my boss at Deutsche Bank said. At that time, there was a biotech conference going on in Boston. "Go get on a plane today," she said. "Go home, pack, get on a plane today and go find out what the f--- is going on. Call me when you get there, and tell me what stocks to start buying."

So that night I got to Boston, and I didn't have the guts to tell her that after art, biology was my worst subject by far. So, I bought a few textbooks and I started to read. I effectively taught myself molecular biology and genomics.

That's what began my career-long love affair with biotechnology, which has been very, very fruitful both career-wise and personally. I've always invested an enormous amount of my capital into various biotechnology firms. I do this based on understanding the technology, what it could do and, more important than anything, the psychology that underpins what happens in the marketplace. That's where I got the full education of what really matters in the stock market.

It was a huge break for me. Getting this job as an analyst and then having this hot sector just land in my lap was huge because, really, nobody wanted to touch it. It was brand new and involved scientific work. So that was an enormous break. It was my Dubai.

Obviously, in 1999 the stock markets were peaking, the tech bubble was rampant and then there was this biotech bubble that was even more inflated by the end of 1999. This is where I started to use what I was learning from practical experience instead of what I had been taught in all my years of education — which was not useful for making money in the market.

Why Stocks Go Up Most of the Time, but Fall Sometimes

When managing money professionally, you're required to constantly keep buying. You're never really allowed to be bearish. In 1999, with my personal money, I was starting to get bearish on stocks. Yet, at work, we were still buying stocks for our mutual funds and stuff like that. As one CEO, Chuck Prince from Citigroup, said during the 2008 crisis: "As long as the music is playing, you've gotta keep dancing."

That's the nature of the financial markets, every mutual fund and pretty much every hedge fund, too. As long as the markets are going up, you can't really be in cash, even though you might think the market is overvalued. There's a game on, and you've got to play.

Making money is hard. When I told people I was a professional investment analyst, a lot of retail (individual) investors would brag: "Well, I made 150% in my account last year," or "I made 600%" on some dot-com stock or something like that.

The number of people who would tell me similar experiences was multiplying. Wherever you went, people would regale you with stories of how much money they had made in the market. While it may seem like a great sign, it's actually always a sign of trouble. As wily Wall Street operator Joseph Kennedy said back in 1929: "You know it is time to sell when shoeshine boys start giving you stock tips." The dumb money, always late to the party, is what drives the stock market higher. That always ends in a crash of some sort.

Now, I'm my father's son. Calculated risk-taking is part of my philosophy when it comes to investing and trading. It's how I made money for clients while on Wall Street. It's how I invest my own money now.

A calculated risk in the financial markets means you take opportunities when the odds are in your favor. That way, when you invest, you have a good chance of making money. You never get a guarantee, of course, but when I get good odds, I make the bet. The key is understanding what is a true calculated risk.

So, why do stocks fall from time to time? What goes wrong? Some of the reasons are downright dirty ... especially at the management level. Effectively, most CEOs are full-time stock promoters — not managers. They dangle a picture of what analysts and investors want to see, and they say all the right things to get you to invest. It can be smoke and mirrors.

If you go back and read the history of the stock market from the 1900s, the era of triumph and optimists, you'll often see the word "promoter." It's gone from the lexicon of the financial markets today, but it does strongly define the role of a CEO. They walk around pitching the stock to various people on Wall Street every day. They used to pitch to me like pharmaceutical reps pitch to doctors. Literally every single day, they'd walk around with slide decks. (Today they probably walk around with iPads.) They would give these presentations on the stock six, eight, 10 times a day, just walking around Wall Street. Then they'd hit the conference circuit.

That's the untold secret of Wall Street, too. For the vast majority of CEOs who show up on CNBC, this is their life. This is what they do every day. Their job, effectively, is to go promote themselves and their company. Keep current investors in and try to get the next investor to come in. Being on TV and all that stuff is part of generating enough PR to keep their name in play.

Take for example Apple CEO Tim Cook. He became CEO in 2011 and is well-known as a promoter. Cook is always trying to get people to buy Apple stock by touting its so-called innovation. When all he's done in the time he's been at Apple is introduce phones in new colors and sizes, while selling massive amounts of stock.

I've also seen this up close. When I worked at the mutual fund division of ING Group, the CEO of one biotech I covered was an Indian guy. Back then, it was a very unusual thing to see an Indian guy, and I got taken.

He said: "Sales are going to be great. Everything is going to be good." The investment bank that was bringing them around clearly was orchestrating things the way portfolio managers and analysts love to see them ... that the stock was going up in tiny little increments every day. You felt a little bit more confident, and that made you put in a little bit more money.

It's the sort of system that momentum and small-cap managers all like to see. So that went on for a few months. We built a sizeable stake, around 2%, in our small-cap fund. It was doing well; I was feeling great. Then, one day, I was at a conference and the company announced absolutely awful results. The stock dropped 50%. FIFTY percent!

I tell you, at that moment I wanted to take a plane ticket back to India rather than go face my boss. We had pagers we would all carry. If you got a message from the boss, you had to reply in real time. She wrote me this terse message: "You come in and see me when you get back."

I was like: "Oh, God." So, I came back in after an entire day of listening to companies essentially pitch themselves at me, taking notes and whatever. I walked into her office at about 5:30 p.m., with a two-hour day still ahead of me, writing my notes up.

As I walked into her office, she asked: "What happened with this company?"

I told her: "The guy lied to me. This is what he told me." Obviously, I didn't do all the right checks. I didn't call pharmacists around the country to see if the drug was actually selling. And my biggest mistake: I took the CEO at his word.

Essentially, they had cooked the books. They had accumulated sales that they didn't really have. She kind of yelled at me for about a minute. I sat there a little longer and then she just said: "Get out of my office."

It was a big, painful hit to the portfolio and just as big a lesson personally. It dinged the fund for sure. But it also woke me up to many things. Number one, obviously, was the real-world impact on the fund. But I always took it a step further and thought: Wow, every person who put their money into this fund also got hurt. That was a powerful hit to my gut.

I felt like I owed them something. I made a mistake, and they suffered for it. It also taught me a great deal, like the things I'd read in history books about scams on Wall Street, how management will trick you and all the games that are played. Here, as a young stock analyst, I had been absolutely taken advantage of. The investment bank and company management had orchestrated something close to fraud, even if nobody was ever made accountable for it.

Effectively, they had set up a scheme to create a picture of what analysts and investors wanted to see and said all the right things that got you to invest. They knew that their sales weren't real. They knew that their accounts receivable was running out. They knew what the inventory position was, and that at least some of the sales figures were a complete sham.

For me, it was a learning experience about how you can analyze a company endlessly, but that you still have to pay close attention to the human element of the market. That's when I really started to focus all my energy toward understanding what the markets were in reality.

Eventually, of course, the dot-com stocks and biotechs flamed out. They laid all of us off, and they gave us packages that are mind-boggling for the average person. I was given one year's severance. I was paid a prorated amount of a bonus I was guaranteed. And they paid for my health care for one year. It was a difficult way to leave a company where I learned so much, but it also was a catalyst that took me down the road that led to where I am today.

Behavior Finance: Unlearning
What College Finance Taught Me

Now unemployed, I had an elite search firm to help me find a new job, but by then, I had chosen not to return to Wall Street. Instead I actually became a hermit. I got a really cheap apartment in New York and refocused my career goals. I ended up reading a great book titled "Beyond Greed and Fear: Understanding Behavioral Finance and the Psychology of Investing," by a man named Hersh Shefrin. It extended my knowledge of this world of behavioral finance, which examines how prices are based on what human beings choose to do versus being based on value. Efficient market theory was hogwash, plain and simple.

Even then in New York, I was able to live cheaply. I probably could have lived for a decade or longer without going back to work. It was not just the amount of money I had. I was 32; I didn't have a family, and I didn't have any debt. I had made a decent amount of money for a while. My own speculative short selling was working. I made money when everybody was losing money in 2002. I didn't have a million dollars or anything like that, but I comfortably had six figures. Looking at my numbers, I couldn't help but think: "Wow, I could live here for 15 years, and I could plausibly even just live cheaply and retire like this." You might say I was one of the earliest to consider the FIRE idea, the whole "financial independence retire early" trend.

But I was still fascinated by the markets. I wrote an investment blog, which I called "Capuchinomics," where I explored all my newfound understanding of markets. My writing was well-received, but it was not really a business that could scale into anything real. So, I put a call in to some of my ex-colleagues who were still on Wall Street to see if anyone was looking for an analyst.

I eventually went to work for a hedge fund, which is really different from a standard Wall Street shop. At the time, these were much more hands-on operations and much less trusting of the numbers fed to them by management. The point of a hedge fund, really, is to grow when the market grows but not lose money when there's a reversal. It was a refreshing change, for sure. I could finally be less beholden to the story I was being told by the management and more responsible for actual results for the client.

When I joined the operation, it was managing $1 billion. My job was to go speak to investors and pitch the fund and private accounts we managed, as well as the mutual funds. Eventually, the hedge fund grew to be a $6 billion fund at its peak, in 2007, and I was proud to have helped it grow. The affiliated asset management company had about $25 billion at the peak, and I was one of the two senior portfolio managers there. In a very hands-on way, since it was a small and nimble shop, I did everything — managed money, talked to clients and was a salesman. I performed every aspect of money management possible.

Folks began to take notice. Our fund was the toast of Wall Street for a while. I was invited to speak at conferences and hobnob with bigwigs. As a result of how well our hedge fund was doing, we kept getting exclusive invites. I remember at one conference in San Francisco, there were so many people who were interested in our fund that it was standing room only.

We were also named one of the "world's best" funds by Barron's. After that, a prestigious private foundation invited me to take part in an investment competition among managers that it hosted.

The foundation wanted to see what we could do with $50 million. At first, a small group of us invited were thrilled to get the money. However, as 2008 unfolded, it became something that no one — including those of us from my firm — wanted to touch. Finally, the folks that ran the fund asked me to handle it. For me, that felt like the moment I had been training for my entire life.

Those were the days when the last thing you wanted to do was come into work, let alone come up with stocks to buy. Then, have the courage of your convictions to actually put your money where your mouth is.

Still, thinking of how my dad would do things, I concluded that the odds were good. Sooner rather than later, the crisis would ebb and the stocks would go up.

We started buying stocks daily in 2008, and we kept buying until 2009. We did it this way, because I had no idea when the exact bottom would come. However, I knew it was close. The market would sometimes drop 5% and even 10% on some days. It could not continue to fall that way.

To keep things in perspective on these really bad days, I'd do a mock days-to-zero counter — imagining how many days it would be if the market kept going down at that rate. At one time, it was down so much it was like seven or eight days until the stock market was theoretically worthless.

Well, I'm happy to say I made a 76% return — during the 2008 to 2009 economic crisis — and won the competition.

I found trading in difficult markets practically second nature. I began to understand innately that human beings are largely driven by things that are not really rational. Shefrin cites example after example of how people have lost money, how people make money and that underpinning this are all the basic principles of speculation.

The best traders and fund managers all use these tactics, such as letting your winners run and cutting your losers off early or buying when there's "blood in the streets." In other words, you buy when the odds are good. You don't just look at the fundamentals alone. You consider how other investors are acting toward a stock.

The fancy term for all this stuff today is "behavioral finance," a field that began in psychology and worked its way into finance. In a way, academia acknowledges that efficient market theory is kind of bull. Ultimately, the stock market runs on human beings making decisions based on emotion and impulses.

The critical impulses in trading are always extremes of fear and greed. That's when I began to see that underpinning the markets was this enormous real estate bubble that was beginning to form in the United States. There was something underneath it that was even bigger. I just couldn't get my hands around it. Now, in hindsight, we know what it was. It was the shadow banking system — derivatives, mortgage-backed bonds and all that.

In the middle of 2008, I woke up and said: "Wait a second. I know what's going on here. This is exactly what I was writing about from 2003 to 2006 in my blogs."

It was during this time, when I was living as a hermit, where I explored all my newfound understanding of markets. I applied them to the massive real estate bubble. Because I had done all the work to understand, the 2008 crisis and scenarios I had been writing about where all coming true. So, I was prepared to deal with the ugliness of that time.

I knew the real estate bubble was imploding and that it was going to take the financial system with it. I tried to persuade the hedge fund's owners that we should be selling our stuff, especially any financial stuff, and that we should reduce our leverage. I knew there was not a chance in hell of making them go short because they were living in a different reality in terms of what the markets and what stocks were back then. But the light has already gone on in my head. "Wait a second," I thought. "I understand exactly what's going on here."

Unable to convince my partners, I essentially said to myself: "I need to get ahead of my redemptions." Redemptions happen when investors want their cash back immediately. People were panicking and demanding their money back from the fund, which meant I was forced to sell to raise that cash. I wanted to get every financial company out of the portfolio as soon as possible, but there was no more liquidity in the markets. It wasn't pleasant work; it wasn't fun. It was incredibly stressful.

While it wasn't easy, we survived. The redemption cycle for us ended by September or October of 2008. We stopped seeing redemptions, and I remember distinctly thinking: "OK, the rush is over." We didn't even see additional redemptions in February of 2009, even though markets were making new lows. You could tell, if you were managing money, that a bottom was near.

My Own Skin in the Game

As it happens, the market bottomed in March of 2009. As a manager, you could feel that something new was coming. Some new event was going to occur that nobody else would know about, let alone understand. In September of 2008, when redemptions started to slow, I started to buy hand over fist in my personal accounts. I took every dollar that I had and started to buy stocks. I actually borrowed money to buy stocks. I leveraged that amount up, and I was completely margined out by the end of 2008 before the market bottomed out.

It was blood in the streets. Even if most of the big funds were afraid to invest, I saw the opportunity right in front of me. Like my dad buying those Indian government bonds, I saw the once-in-a-lifetime trade, in real time, and I took it.

By the end of 2008, I think every single stock that I bought was down 50%, some 60%. Just to give some personal context as to what was going on while this was happening, I had my first child in January of 2008. So I'm selling all this stuff to get ahead of redemptions, and all the clients wanted to get out. But in my personal investing, I'm doing the reverse. I couldn't persuade my clients to do the same. Very few clients cared to put any money into stocks.

But I couldn't buy fast enough. At one point in time, even though I could see the redemptions had stopped, even to me it felt like: "God, I think I'm about to go bankrupt here."

Virtually everything I owned was down. I remember telling my family sometime in February, just before the bottom: "You know, if this doesn't turn around, we're going to be eating rice and beans. We're done. We're cooked." I said: "I've taken everything we have and bet it, and I don't know what's next. I feel like everything that I know and I understand tells me that this is what I should do, but I don't know."

Within a few days, of course, the markets bottomed out and stocks started to go up, beginning a multiyear bull market. I owned tiny startup stocks such as Netflix and Whole Foods. I didn't buy "safe" names such as Coca-Cola. I even bought junk stocks because I knew from previous experience that into the first ascent after a crash, the stuff that goes up is the stuff that has the least liquidity. Small, junky stocks go up first. So that's what I was doing personally. As the stock market was going up, I began to be able to see that it was going to work out OK. It was going to be all right, in terms of my personal stuff and for the fund, too.

I remember telling my family: "We're leaving." So, we chose between a few different places, then came down to North Carolina. As soon as we got there, we knew immediately this was going to be our new home. On our second visit here, we bought a house.

Helping Ordinary Investors Live Comfortably

Fast forward to today: I'm still living in North Carolina, and I'm still an investor. Investing has been ingrained in my mind since I was a child, when my father explained to me that it was the best way to get out of India's rat race, where few escape the lower class.

Perhaps that's why today, investing has taken a unique turn for me. When I was on Wall Street, I made money for the 1%, the European aristocracy, Swiss private banks and the Royal Bank of Scotland. My job was to help big banks turn millions into billions.

But I knew that wasn't how I wanted to spend the rest of my career. I wanted to help Main Street Americans find ways to turn thousands into hundreds of thousands and enjoy life. That's precisely why I started writing my own newsletter, *Profits Unlimited*, and then this book designed to give everyday folks access to the wealth opportunities that Wall Street doesn't want revealed.

It truly all goes back to my dad. One day when I was in Mumbai with my dad, we saw a few people digging a hole. There was one guy in particular who was standing around while the rest of the people were digging.

My dad said to me: "Do you know who makes more money, the guy digging the hole or the guy standing there directing where they should dig the hole?" I don't know what I answered, but I do remember what he said next: "If you don't study, you're going to end up being the guy digging the hole. The people who get educated and who use their brains, they're the ones that stand around telling other people what to do."

That always stuck in my head: that the way forward was with my brains and not my physique or physical strength. I look at stocks the same way. You can use your brains to make money, and if you do it well you can make a lot from the same initial effort.

And once you have some money, I say spend it. So many people believe they need to hold their stocks forever. Personally, my philosophy is that when you make money in stocks, use your returns for something useful. For example, I've used gains to buy houses, land, cars and vacations. Sadly, my father had money but never enjoyed his life, and on Wall Street so many of my business associates never used their profits to enjoy their lives.

That's a shame because life isn't permanent. No one knows the future for certain, so, for me, a good experience is worth a lot. The whole point of having money or wealth is to make our lives a bit better.

So, it makes sense to sell your stocks when you have gains from time to time. Use your gains to buy a house, a car, a vacation or to pay for college. Buy your sweetheart a beautiful gift. Because you can't eat your stocks or live in them. You can't hug your stocks. And they won't love you back.

Stocks are just a means to an end, and our time is more valuable than any stock. Wall Street doesn't want you to follow this advice, of course. Big brokers and fund managers want to get rich off of your money. On Wall Street, you know your company is minting money when it throws a fancy Christmas party. In good years, it'll be at the fanciest restaurants or hotels. Limousines take you to and from the party. The finest steak, $500 bottles of wine and $100 cigars are served. After the regular party, exclusive after-parties pop up, and only a few select employees who make the big bucks are invited.

At the after-parties, there's just one topic of conversation: bonuses. Asset managers, brokers and analysts (aka Wall Streeters) live for their year-end bonuses. That's where someone can make three or four times their regular salary in a good year. In a great year, it might be as much as 10 or 20 times their regular salary.

To be truthful, this kind of swag never did much for me. Don't get me wrong. I enjoy nice things. But the "rewards" were never the thing that drove me on Wall Street. For me, Wall Street was something that had fascinated me from the time I was a kid growing up in India. I revered the rock-solid traders of old who knew how to make money for their customers and for themselves.

But the old Wall Street from when I was a kid is completely gone. Back then, you made money buying low and selling high. It took work, guts and sound judgment. And that's all gone.

In its place is another kind of Wall Street, which makes money in a bad way. It takes advantage of customers, ripping them off each and every single day. Wall Streeters get rich today by charging customers fees and commissions. The price tags seem small. However, it adds up.

For example, mutual funds — like the ones in your 401(k) — will charge you as much as 1% or 2% for managing your money. That doesn't sound like a lot. But over time, it's a difference of hundreds of thousands of dollars filling your mutual fund manager's bank account instead of yours. Then, let's say, you let Wall Street in. They'll charge you 1% or even 0.5% for managing your money — which are pretty standard levels.

This is the "Wall Street money suck," and it absolutely does suck. Bottom line: Avoid Wall Street and you can get to $2.3 million. With Wall Street, you'll lose as much as 26% of your savings to fees. This is why I don't own a single mutual fund or hedge fund. It's also why I tell anyone who will listen to get out of high-cost mutual funds.

Sadly, few people listen, because most people get suckered in by Wall Street's pitch, many times because of the fear of not knowing what to do. This is another reason I started my own *Profits Unlimited* newsletter. Remember, I was on Wall Street and I managed mutual funds, so I know what I'm talking about. Wall Street claims it deserves the money it sucks out of your account because asset managers beat the market.

In other words, they claim to earn it. Remember those old investment manager ads on TV? The Smith Barney ads with actor John Houseman, looking like Winston Churchill in his three-piece suit, would intone: "They make money the old-fashioned way. They earn it." That's also long gone.

The truth is, most Wall Street funds lose against the market. In fact, Standard & Poor's reported that just two out of the 2,862 mutual funds are beating the S&P 500 Index for the current bull market that began in March 2009. That's terrible!

Despite this horrible performance, people still have around $20 trillion invested in the top 10 mutual funds and similar investments. I told you earlier that Wall Street's fees and commissions only seem small. Let's do the math on $18.2 trillion. At 1%, Wall Street sucks in $182 billion per year. Remember, Wall Street does nothing special for this. What Wall Street offers is no different than what your electricity company or water company offers you. It's just another service.

Would you pay more to get power from one power outlet versus another, when the quality of the power is identical? Or would you pay more for your groceries going through check-out lane No. 1 versus check-out lane No. 2 (and you don't get through it any faster)? You wouldn't, because you understand that it's a rip-off. And you shouldn't get ripped off by Wall Street when it attempts to charge you exorbitant fees.

The truth is: You don't need Wall Street to make money in the stock market. In the following pages, I'll show you how to use my Rules of the Game for success in the stock market without needing Wall Street. And with the coming bull market, there's never been a better time to start.

PART
-2-

How to Capitalize on a Life-Changing Bull Market

What Ordinary Investors Do Wrong That Holds Them Back

I am, ultimately, an insider gone rogue.

Fact is, I never did fit in on Wall Street. I quickly grew tired of the corporate greed and the 16-hour workdays that took me away from my family and a balance of life. So, I walked away when I knew we had plenty to live on. Now, I have the privilege of taking my children to school and watching them take piano and fencing lessons — things my family could never afford when I was a kid. And I can focus my attention on what I do love about investing and help others profit, sidestepping the Wall Street and corporate greed.

The first thing to understand is that markets are driven by emotions, above all. Markets are made of investors, and investors are human beings. Full stop. That means most are emotional investors, to their own detriment. They let fear drive them. And Wall Street insiders prey on it, and profit from it. But fear isn't the only emotional market driver.

John Templeton, the late billionaire who founded Templeton Funds, made his first millions buying stocks in 1939 — even bankrupt companies — as World War II was just getting started. Templeton understood that great bull markets are born of pessimism, built on skepticism, mature on optimism and always end in euphoria.

That euphoria moment is the most dangerous. In 1999, it was tech stocks and biotech stocks. In 2007, it was houses. Everybody was telling you how many houses they owned. It's psychological. We are our own worst enemies when it comes to investing because we are human. We can't help ourselves. But knowing this essential truth about human nature is the first step to overcoming it and prospering.

Start off Small, It's the Best Way to Stay Humble

In addition to investing emotionally and focusing on value investing, many people wrongly think they can't invest because they don't have enough money to get started. The thing is, most do have enough.

Looking back, when I began investing, I only had $200 in my very first brokerage account. So, starting with a small amount of money is not only doable, it's actually common. The thing you want to keep in mind, though, is that you don't want to put all of your funds into just one or two stocks — which you'll be tempted to do if you're starting out with a small sum of money.

The reason this is a bad idea is because if you end up taking a large loss, you're going to end up losing a lot of your "seed" money, or the amount of money you started with. You also don't want to be discouraged. In the investing world, you have to be prepared for losses, as well as gains.

The second problem is that you can't know which stock is going to go up first, or by the highest amount. In other words, you want to give yourself a good chance of catching a big winner — a stock that goes up a lot.

So, what I'd do is take $1,000 and split it across at least four or five stocks, putting $200 to $250 into each recommendation. This way you'll limit your losses and maximize your chance of getting a large winner.

In time, you begin to reinvest your gains, so you're playing now with what I call "house money." It's like your safety net. Kind of like when you make a $50 bet and are up in your winnings. That's when you pocket your original $50 and just play with the money you've won. That takes off a lot of the stress of investing, which in turn helps you stay focused.

Another common mistake many investors make is that they buy stocks that they already know. For example, they buy stocks of a big company they've heard of, such as IBM or General Electric. Those are the stocks that they gravitate to, even though there are more than 3,000 stocks that you can buy. Since people tend to own the stocks that they are familiar with and that they know, that leaves them out of fast-growing, new stocks that can go up a lot. A whole lot!

Investors also like to focus on stocks with a low nominal price. For example, if a stock has a $10 price, they like it. Meanwhile, they're hesitant or won't buy a stock with a $100 price. That's because people can imagine a $10 stock perhaps going to $100, but it's a little bit harder for them to imagine a $100 stock going to $1,000.

This is why stocks "split" when prices get above $100 a share. It's to attract investors who are biased against an "expensive" stock, which is most investors.

Nevertheless, the truth is that the stock pricing by itself really doesn't tell you what a stock is going to do. A $10 stock in a low-growth industry with a bad business model can go down to $2 or even $1. My personal experience has been that a low-priced stock often represents a bad business, so limiting yourself to them means you often put yourself into businesses that are quite poor and where you have actually a smaller chance of doing well.

If you look at companies such as Google or Amazon, these stocks have higher prices and have gone above $1,000. In other words, these represented fast-growing businesses with really good products and services that gave you a much better chance of making money. When a stock goes from $10 to $100, you're making $90. If a stock goes from $100 to $1,000, you're making the same percentage, but a lot more money. That's why I recommend investing in stocks on the basis of growth in the business itself, not price.

Another thing I would tell you to focus on is market cap. That's because market capitalization represents the size of the company. A $300 million company that has great products and services can quickly go to $600 million, and then to $1.2 billion, and then just keep doubling again and again. That's what I really focus on when selecting stocks.

Here are a few personal examples.

I discovered Sarepta Therapeutics when it was in the infancy stage of developing a drug to treat muscular dystrophy. That's the stage where people are past learning about it and are now implementing concrete plans to use it. I invested in the company and made a gain of 2,539%.

I was also an early investor in Netflix. While most people were skeptical of Netflix in 2008, I wasn't. Having insight on technological advancements, I knew the future of television was streaming online video. I invested and made gains of 329%.

I also saw a huge opportunity in Universal Display when it created organic LED technology. I recognized the opportunity early on and pocketed gains of 293%.

Another company I bought into on the ground floor was Google. I jumped on its initial public offering (IPO) — despite a huge amount of negative sentiment surrounding the stock — and more than doubled my investment. Since its IPO, Google's stock has shot up a whopping 2,271%! I sold out of it before Google hit its peak. Many people have asked why. The truth is, I sold it because I needed the money.

And that's true for other stocks that I was early to invest in, such as Netflix. As I've said, I believe in using gains from the stock market to make life better. Even though I got in early on Google and other stocks, I also sold them fairly early to do the things that I wanted to do. And I believe this is the best way to make the markets work for you — to improve your life and the lives of your loved ones. And the goal of this book is to help you do precisely that.

Throughout this book I will give you a solid understanding of how stock markets really work. I will begin by telling you why I believe that the bull market of a generation is still ahead of us, and why you should invest now.

Sure, a stock market correction is always in the cards. But the strategic investor is always focused on what's ahead and how to profit from it.

Teaching you those skills is the reason for this book, and I'm excited to help you learn how to win at investing in any market, even difficult markets we will surely face.

Why Stocks Always Win
vs. Other Investments

In the long run, stocks are the biggest winners for investors. The stock market delivers nearly four times over what other investments offer. Mainly because of the economy, reinvesting of dividends and compounding over time. The data shows that stocks just crush everything.

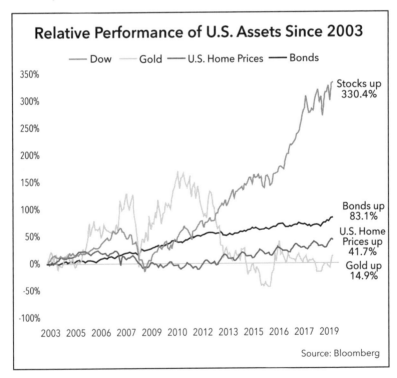

Relative Performance of U.S. Assets Since 2003

—— Dow ——— Gold —— U.S. Home Prices —— Bonds

Stocks up 330.4%

Bonds up 83.1%

U.S. Home Prices up 41.7%

Gold up 14.9%

Source: Bloomberg

Take a look at the relative performance total return gains from the following three asset classes from 2003 to 2019:

- Stocks: 330.4%.

- Bonds: 83.1%

- U.S. Home Price: 41.7%

We know we need stocks to make real money over time. But what makes a bull market durable for decades? Stocks grow faster than the economy itself — fast enough to outstrip inflation, too. But you still need the economy to grow.

If you read the headlines today, you may be scared away from getting into stocks. The negativity is painted all over the front pages of mainstream media.

"Prepare for a big stock market sell-off!"

"The stock market could plunge more than 50%."

"PREPARE FOR THE BIG CRASH."

And even if you see headlines on the opposite spectrum, they don't last. We seem to live in a world where doom and gloom gets more attention. And media loves attention.

Now if you simply dabble in the market from time to time and you see these headlines, you might panic. After all, didn't we have a crash in 2008? A lot of people lost a lot of money back then. So, a lot of people might be thinking: "I should sell everything, clear the decks now."

But in my near-three decades of experience in investing, I can tell you this is the wrong way to think. By now, you know I've managed a LOT of money. So, when you see headlines like these, it really helps to go and look at the facts. And the facts are really, really different — I mean night-and-day different.

Don't Let Fear Trump Facts
in Today's Economy

Now, one of the reasons people are concerned about the market is because of the amount of debt in the economy. But when you look at debt relative to income, we are really nowhere near the level of debt people imagine. Mortgage debt is the greatest amount of debt the average person has, even in retirement. (Secured debt, like a mortgage, by the way, which is very different from, say, unsecured credit card debt.)

When comparing mortgage debt to people's incomes, it's really at a multiyear low. The other thing that people often say is that income hasn't grown in ages. The fact is: Income did go down during the recession that followed the 2008 financial crisis. However, personal incomes are rising at a more rapid rate.

Another concern many people have is that the economy is growing too fast. In 2018, we had our first 4% GDP growth number since 2014 and people's reaction to that was to panic. That reaction tells you about the mood of investors, not the facts on the ground.

I bring up home ownership because of unfounded fears that we're blowing another real estate bubble. In fact, the data from the Federal Reserve shows home ownership is at a very low level, historically. You can't have a bubble when the number of homeowners is so low. For a bubble, people are buying houses a lot to raise the prices. But since the number of homeowners is low, you don't have the demand needed for the bubble. In reality, we really have not even begun to recover from the real estate bubble that burst in 2008.

This matters because in my experience, when you see such a huge divergence between the facts and the collective mood, and the opinions that sway people, it's usually an opportunity. It's usually a time to buy stocks because sooner rather than later you're going to see the stock market go up.

The reason for that is that these headlines reflect panic. They reflect a bearish, pessimistic view of the world. What happens next is that people sell their stocks. With a big sell-off in stocks, prices go down because supply is greater than demand. Then, once the selling is done, investors realize that the news is nowhere near as bad as what was hyped in the headlines.

So, the investors who sold among many others come back into the market and they lift prices up. We want to be positioned for that realization and the resulting bull market to come — to take advantage, and buy in, at the precise moment those stock prices are down for companies with solid business plans that are leveraging growing markets. That way, we benefit when they (inevitably) go back up.

The Future Is Now, Once Again

Coming to the United States was a new beginning for me. Going to college was like diving into a whole new world, where I had to figure out something new each and every day. It forced me to figure things out bit by bit.

So many things that are so obvious today were so hard to figure out on my own back then. For example, I didn't know how to dress for cold weather. Coming from Dubai where the average temperatures range from the 60s at night to highs in the 100s during the day, I was not prepared for the winter snow and freezing temperatures. So, when I came to New Jersey, I was basically cold almost all the time in the winter. I wasn't prepared.

What's going on in the stock market reminds me a lot of that time, because today most people are completely un-prepared. Unless you have experience and knowledge of how markets work, you're very likely going to make all the wrong decisions. And you could end up missing out on something that could completely change your life — such as a bull market in stocks.

Now, when you look back to 1982, you'll find two incredible similarities to the bull market that has been building since 2009. First, there was an incredible technology — the personal computer was just beginning to emerge as an enormous economic force in our economy. Second, you had the coming of age of the baby-boom generation, the oldest of whom had just turned 36.

Today, we have the same two things going on. First, we have this incredible technological development. I'm talking about the Internet of Things, or IoT. It's beginning to revolutionize how our world works in everything from our roads to cars to our health, and every part of our lives. If you are using anything tied to a network (a device, an app, the web), you are a part of the IoT. Second, we have the coming of age of the millennial generation, the biggest generation in U.S. history since the baby boomers.

Now, I understand that you might be skeptical. Especially if you watch all the doom-and-gloom headlines the mainstream media puts out there. However, I've spent a decade researching bull and bear markets throughout history. And this combination of a major technological change and a new generation coming of age is as close as you are going to get to a sure thing in terms of a formula for predicting a major new bull market. And it's one that I'm staking my credibility and reputation on.

Incredible amounts of money can be made in fairly short periods of time. That really doesn't even do justice to how much money was made by some investors during the last major bull market in 2009. There were incredible winners: Microsoft was up 60,000%. Cisco was up 55,000%. Even simpler companies such as The Home Depot were up 45,000%. It represents the combination of a technological development that can be used across companies, at homes and all across the economy, plus the coming of age of a very large generation — one whose spending habits and consumption habits are big enough to move the economy.

That's really why I predict the Dow will hit 50,000. And to me, 50,000 is just the beginning. I expect the Dow to go much higher than that. Why? Consider the Internet of Things and the rise of the millennial generation. The way that I look at it, it's like 1982 today, and we have the same two things going on: We've got this technology, the Internet of Things, which has wide applicability all through the economy and is going to continually increase productivity and increase profits. And then we have this 92 million-strong generation of Americans called millennials who are just rising to their peak earning power and incomes. They're changing the shape of our economy the same way the baby boomers did.

Now, some believe that the U.S. stock market is bound to crash. On August 13, 1979, *BusinessWeek* ran a cover, now infamous, that said: "The Death of Equities." It has now become somewhat of a contrarian indicator when the media makes these big market predictions, because the *BusinessWeek* cover was spectacularly mistimed. In fact, back in 1979, it was actually the perfect moment to start buying stocks. If you started buying stocks on that date, you would have been a tiny bit early, but would have had outstanding gains. Unfortunately, there were so many bad experiences that had happened in the past that affected the way people looked at the future, inflation, foreign crises and so on.

That's where we are today. We went through a horrible crash in 2008. We've been through a polarizing election. There's been trouble in the Middle East and with Russia. There are so many negative things for people to focus on, and that's affecting the way that we're looking at the future. Yet I believe all those worries are, in fact, largely in the past. The Internet of Things is about the future, about a productivity revolution in everything that we do.

I know that to some, all of this seems crazy. However, let's think back to 1982 again, to the beginning of the last major bull market in stocks. People were pessimistic about the future of our country then, too. One easy way to measure the negative mood of that time period is to look at another one of the most popular magazines back then, *Time*.

The September 6, 1982, issue of *Time* featured an image of a bull and the words "Wall Street Olé! The Economy Eh?" It was representing the new bull market that was just beginning. Inside the issue were doubts of the stock market that are similar to the ones that people have today: No one predicted it. No one can explain it. No one dreamed that it could keep going day after day after day. And yet it did — for years into decades. Fortunes were made and made again. The same is true now, and this time we are more equipped to predict it.

People always ask me: "Paul, how do you come up with your investment ideas?"

The second question I get is: "How come so many of your stocks are doing so well even though the stock market is down?"

For me, it really starts like a pyramid. I start in terms of thinking of a theme which comes about from reading a lot of magazines, books, trade journals and online news stories. Through that, I start to put together a picture of a technical development which is now mature enough that it's starting to become a good business, a substantial business, and one that can grow for many years to come. Finally, I narrow it down to the right stock to buy now.

Don't Forget the Simple Secret for Picking Great Stocks

The key to understanding how to pick stocks that go up, ultimately, is to actually go and invest. You might be shocked to know that most people who manage money on Wall Street still don't understand why stocks go up.

Why does one stock go up after you buy it, and why doesn't another stock go up? The real reason isn't going to be discussed by the media or by the phony people who show up on CNBC. They focus on the product. They focus on the CEO. They focus on all this extraneous stuff, but you'll never hear a person actually tell you why a stock is going to go up. Perhaps that's because they don't know.

It's really a very simple thing, which is that somebody is willing to pay a higher price for the stock today versus yesterday. Then somebody else is willing to come and pay an even higher price the day after and the day after. There's only one reason why someone would do that. It's because they believe that the value of that business is growing.

If you don't understand how money flows to different places, then you don't really get the whole picture. My very first Wall Street job was in the back office, and that was useful in its own way because I got a sense of how the plumbing of Wall Street works. The 2008 financial crisis taught me that there's something wrong with the incentives on Wall Street, the huge fees collected by hedge funds and asset management companies while "regular people" — Main Street Americans — lose their money permanently. I didn't want to keep living my life like that.

At some point I just thought: Well, I'm very good at what I do. And I love investing, the research, and finding and creating successful strategies. How should I go about it in the future? Should I continue to work for people who already have an enormous amount of money and make them wealthier, or should I do something that has never really been done? Why not take my expertise, my knowledge, and try to make ordinary people rich instead?

The most valuable thing that I've learned is something simple. I've learned that the way to make money on Wall Street is to focus on the simplest part of it, which is that a stock market is a market. When people think about stocks, they seem to forget common sense — the kind of common sense they would show when they go into a supermarket. When it comes to investing, people put this crazy hat on and they forget the most fundamental thing, which is that you want to buy stocks going up in price.

Now, stocks can go down, too. People often ask me why I sell stocks when they go down instead of buying more. For me, the only true benefit of owning a stock is the fact that it can go up and continue to go up. By that definition, if the stock is going down, it no longer meets my criteria for why I want to own the stock in the first place.

The second reason is that my experience shows me that most times when a stock starts going down, it keeps going down, and it goes down by much more.

Thirdly, my experience also shows me that whatever is wrong with the stock and the company, that problem often lasts much longer than you think, and it's often worse than you imagine. In fact, that's usually why the stock continues to go down.

My way of making sure that I don't buy into these scenarios is to be certain that the company has fixed its problems. The company shows us that by showing that its sales are growing, and that its profits are growing. That way you know you're buying into a stock that is headed up, not down.

PART
-3-

Rules of the Game —
the Secrets to Success
in the Stock Market

How I Pick Stocks

Ten years ago, when I was working at a hedge fund in New York City, I was having the same argument with my colleagues day in and day out. I remember letting them in on a stock that I invested in, which I knew without a shadow of a doubt was about to revolutionize the way that people experienced at-home entertainment.

At first my colleagues were intrigued. They wanted to know what kind of company I believed could more than double its business within the next three years.

But once I told them the name of my investment, all my associates thought I'd lost my mind. They called me crazy. They said that I should sell all my shares immediately if I didn't want to lose every penny I'd invested.

Looking back, I can almost understand why. Wall Street was calling the stock a short — a position created when a trader sells an asset first with the intention of repurchasing it or covering it later at a lower price. Analysts thought heavy competition and slow subscriber growth meant low sales projections. Critics called the company's new business model unnecessary.

But it's never been in my nature to trust what mainstream analysts are saying. For me, it was a learning experience about how you can analyze a company endlessly, but yet you still have to pay close attention to the human element of the market. That's when I really started to focus all my energy toward understanding what the markets were in reality. I knew that my research was sound — and my indicators were flashing "buy!"

So I stayed in the stock, and it's a good thing I did.

I don't want to reveal the exact dollar amount I made. I can tell you that my return on investment was high enough that when I finally sold my shares, I was able to put the money toward a sizable down payment on my house.

But I did get one thing wrong. The company didn't just double its audience during my three-year timeline. It nearly tripled it, going from 7.48 million users in 2007 to 20.01 million users in 2010. And at the end of 2016, it had a customer base of 93.8 million people. One of those might have been you.

See, the stock that I invested in was Netflix.

And while that might seem like a sound investment idea today, 10 years ago I was a black sheep among my peers. Since that time, I've uncovered plenty of other "risky" ventures that investors didn't want to touch. But I knew they were about to take off.

For instance, I bought into a little-known, "down and out" company called Coeur Mining that the financial media was quick to shun. Every technical indicator said that the company was a hopeless investment, yet I ignored Wall Street. I bought in anyway.

To everyone's surprise (except mine), a month after I purchased the stock, Coeur Mining's shares started to tick up. It became a "buy" according to the Bollinger Bands. Then it broke through its 50-day moving average (a sign of stock value that I'll cover in more detail later, when I explain my "GoingUpness" investment strategy).

And it got a green light from both the MACD and RSI. The moving average convergence/divergence, or MACD, is designed to reveal changes in the strength, direction, momentum and duration of a trend in a stock's price. The Relative Strength Indicator, or RSI, is meant to chart the current and historical strength or weakness of a stock or market based on the closing prices of a recent trading period. For me, this confirmed the stock had momentum.

Suddenly, everyone wanted in. But because I knew of Coeur Mining's potential before everyone else, I was able to purchase shares cheaply. That is, right before other investors came in and bid the stock up — boosting the value of my holdings dramatically. I ended up walking away with a 738% gain.

Yet if I had waited for Wall Street and the media to tell me to buy, I would have never made such a high return. After years of fine-tuning and countless trial-and-error tests, I've created a system that specifically targets stocks that only have one way to go — up!

The Heart of Every Explosive Stock Pick

While there are a handful of strategies that investors use to predict which stocks to pick, I feel like I have developed the best one. And my numbers — as you read above — prove it works. The first component to picking winning stocks is something I call "true momentum." The second piece of the puzzle is what I call "GoingUpness."

Companies with true momentum could be very different from one another. It could be a social media company, a pharmaceutical drug company, even a robotics maker.

On the surface, none of these businesses will appear to have anything in common. Yet each stock will share one very important characteristic: They must all be showing signs of extreme acceleration in the growth rate of their business.

That's the core of what it means for a stock to have true momentum. It's really that simple. How you find each of these companies, however, is much more complex — and difficult to explain.

See, my strategy acts like an X-ray machine. It's capable of seeing through all the surface layers of a stock to reveal the real story underneath. It ignores what Wall Street is telling you to do.

It shuts out all the gossip from the media. And it even goes beyond the technical analysis of the stock price.

Other technical traders will spend time trying to figure out if a stock's price will go up or down. And that's fine if you're looking to make a quick return in the market. But that's simple, shallow research compared to all the indicators that I look at because, frankly, I'm in this to make big gains.

I want to turn thousands into hundreds of thousands, and hundreds of thousands into millions. But to do that, I have to analyze the true momentum of every single potential investment to determine if the company has true momentum.

So, no matter how much I might like a business, its current market or its future potential, if I don't see immediate signs that it has true momentum, then I'm not going to invest in it — at least not at that time.

But to find stocks that have signs of extreme growth acceleration, I have to look at dozens of indicators.

These include things like gross and net revenue, earnings, debt, current assets, operating cash flow, market sector, earnings before interest, tax, depreciation and amortization (EBITDA), insider ownership and consumer need for the product or service. The list goes on and on.

In fact, the full list of indicators is much, much larger than that. Therein lies the difficulty in determining which stocks are showing signs of real true momentum. There is no set number that you can track that will tell you when to invest, or when it's time to get out of the stock.

My colleagues at my hedge fund didn't see the massive potential that Netflix was presenting to investors on a silver platter. That's surprising because these were very well-respected financial analysts who had years of experience under their belts and who knew how the industry worked. So, for the everyday investor, spotting a company with true momentum is a monumental challenge.

And that's because it requires the perfect set of circumstances for both the company and the investor to succeed.

To explain this a bit further, let's go back in time.

How I Knew Netflix Was a Buy

I mentioned Netflix earlier, but let me tell you the story behind how I found that flashing buy.

When Netflix first came onto the scene in 1997, it was only an online DVD rental service with just 1,000 DVD titles for people to choose from. You may recall its first service, which was to send DVDs through the mail. But the company always had grander plans than that in the works.

Aiming for convenience, founder and CEO, Reed Hastings, knew that the future of Netflix didn't involve shipping physical discs to people's homes. At one point he even said: "Because DVD is not a hundred-year format, people wonder what will Netflix's second act be." As it would turn out, that second act was online video streaming.

But while the way forward was clear to the company, the path to get there was littered with obstacles. At the time, Blockbuster stood in the way as a huge competitor. With thousands of retail locations, a massive customer base and a trusted business model, many people wondered what benefits Netflix could offer that Blockbuster couldn't.

On top of that, when the company first started out, the technology to stream videos wasn't quite there. The bandwidth wasn't strong enough for videos to come in clearly without freezing. And there was the constant threat that larger digital cable companies like Comcast or Verizon might steal customers with their video on demand services.

In fact, I remember when one of my colleagues asked me this question: "If you want to watch a movie at home and not go out to get it, why wouldn't you just use pay-per-view?"

Whenever someone starts a counterargument with the words "Why wouldn't you?" that's my cue that they haven't researched the topic at hand and that I'm actually onto something really good. And it turns out that I was correct.

Netflix went full steam ahead and disrupted its own business model, and reinvented itself into an internet-based movie distributor. It didn't take long for the service to gain momentum. Its streaming service got faster as the internet advanced.

Its subscriber base started to grow rapidly, drawing customers in with its low-cost streaming delivery. The concept of late fees was no more.

The shift was a major success. In just a few years' time, the company's subscriber base nearly tripled and it has continued to ramp up from there. It was also able to keep its operating costs at a minimum because of not having to maintain physical store locations with thousands of employees. As a result, its revenue began to surge.

The more I tracked Netflix, the more I liked the company. And when I heard of its plans to move its content online, I knew I was looking at something revolutionary.

See, part of identifying true momentum comes down to understanding when it makes sense for a company to change its business structure. It's this rapid change in structure that tells me the company is setting itself up for a massive new surge in growth, which means that the stock is soon going to profit from huge gains.

This point of rapid expansion is what I refer to as the Pinnacle Moment. It's my cue that the company has built its business out and is ready to grow.

Often this comes at a company's "second stage" of development. This is where the company has already established itself before its newest expansion venture, and has experienced an initial growth spurt.

What gets difficult is determining whether or not a business is actually at this pinnacle point.

Many companies try to revitalize themselves and fail. It requires constant monitoring and careful consideration of each one of my indicators to determine whether or not a stock is a good investment.

Now, don't get me wrong. I'm not perfect. While I would love for my strategy to work every single time and find the stocks that will be absolutely phenomenal winners, every now and then one is going to fall short. But the number of big winners that I've experienced in my long trading career shows that we're going to get more right than we do wrong.

Targeting Massive Winners that Will Beat Warren Buffett's Portfolio

The main goal is simple: to target stocks that are on the verge of taking off. How?

Once you identify stocks with true momentum, you use my GoingUpness strategy to target the right *time* to buy in. I'll tell you exactly how in the next section. This one-two punch strategy looks for stocks that have explosive potential and pinpoints the right time to buy. Ones that would beat out Warren Buffett's old-world stocks. That's how to generate the big gains. Let me explain.

Warren Buffett is a legend in the investing world. But he is slacking when it comes to new-world stocks, clinging tightly to old-world "zombie stocks."

Buffett invested in companies like Coca-Cola, Kraft and many insurance companies, thinking that they capture people's daily habits, but now his portfolio is filled with stock zombies. Every day, Buffett's investments die more and more, either slowly or quickly. And there are three main reasons why I believe Buffett is falling short of the mark.

First, we're currently in a new era of healthier consumer preferences. Where once people saw Coca-Cola as just another refreshing drink, we now see sugary drinks as drivers of obesity and diabetes. Owning stocks that don't match what the majority of people value can be detrimental to a portfolio.

Then, consider that new tech is setting up to wipe out many industries, such as insurance as we know it. New fintech and insurance companies are changing the way insurance is written, priced and sold.

Based on my research, these companies are disrupting the old ways to become the new market leaders. Lemonade, Square, PayPal and crypto companies are all changing the game, meaning that stocks like Wells Fargo will slowly lose market share.

Finally, despite his best efforts to invest in tech with Apple, Buffett just joined the tech train a little too late. With all of the new tech initial public offerings (IPOs) joining the market, the old-world stocks will soon be eclipsed by them — upsetting the Apple cart, so to speak.

From artificial intelligence to biotech to the Internet of Things (IoT), there are plenty of new-industry tech stocks entering the market that are ready to overtake their competition. I'll show you exactly what I mean later in this book when I tell you about the big mega trends that are transforming our world.

This disruption is a huge part of every sector of our economy. Simply put, the world of finance is about to shift into the future, and Warren Buffett's portfolio is nowhere near ready. Right now, Buffett's portfolio is filled with insurance and bank stocks — basically, everything that fintech stocks are about to swallow whole.

By staying all in on these old-world stocks, Buffett has set himself up for disaster once the tsunami of new-world companies starts to dominate the financial market.

And we are still at the forefront of these trends — before many realize how massive the opportunities are — which is where I foresee a lot of investing opportunities.

You now know the first step in finding the winners is to identify stocks with true momentum potential. Now let me tell you the second part of the equation ... GoingUpness.

Grab Winners on the Way Up — My "GoingUpness" System

The essence of my GoingUpness system is based on this: Most people just want to buy a stock and see it go up. That's what every investor and reader I've ever met has told me. The sooner the stock goes up, the better.

That's my desire, too. Instead of investing in a stock for the dividends or because I love the company's product, I do it simply to make big money. Small gains of 5% or even 10% don't do anything for me — big, life-changing gains are what I want. And I want to pocket those gains soon — within a year of investing. So, I look for stocks that have explosive growth potential.

As I mentioned, one of the areas with the biggest growth prospects today is the Internet of Things. It's the next great wave of development that will shape the internet, and it's my main investment focus right now. The first wave was the "Internet of People," which enabled people to connect with other people and businesses. The Internet of Things, on the other hand, will connect machines with other machines. What sets it apart from the internet we currently use is that it's going to connect and collect data from absolutely everything — driverless cars, smart TVs and fridges, internet-enabled thermostats, wearable devices like Fitbits, not to mention millions of industrial, scientific and supply chain applications. The innovations are endless. And they stand to revolutionize the way we live.

That's why we want to get in now, at the forefront of new technological achievements before anyone else realizes how massive the opportunities are. To do that, we're going to use my system.

So how do we use the GoingUpness system to make big gains? Well, it's a matter of understanding supply and demand.

Take Google as an example. I knew Google was a solid stock because all day, every day, I used the search engine to research stocks. Google made it easy to learn anything I wanted to know, something we take for granted now.

But searching the internet wasn't easy at first. Before Google, searching the internet was, frankly, horrible. I could spend days looking for something. The biggest website in the world was Yahoo!, and the supposed innovation of the time was a kludgy, exasperating human-created index of the web. It was useful for finding, say, a few websites about buying a car or taking a vacation. But it was useless if your search was more detailed or expansive.

With Google, finding very specific information went from taking days or weeks to minutes. As an investor, I would have gladly paid hundreds and even thousands of dollars for the speed, accuracy and ease of using the search engine over blindly piecing together where things might be online.

Yet, amazingly, there was unrelenting pessimism and negativity about the stock as Google prepared to go public in 2004. It had found a way to launch its IPO without paying exorbitant fees, and investment bankers hated it. In turn, investors became nervous, and many traders who were going to buy the stock chickened out. In other words, the demand for Google's IPO was down — but for no good reason. It was all due to media negativity.

Today, that's something I look for in my stock picks: Is demand for shares down, and is that reaction unreasonable? Once I check that off the list, I look at the supply angle. For example, Google was originally planning to sell shares at $135. Then the price was cut to $110, then $95. By August 19, 2004, the day Google went public, the price was down to $85 — a last-minute 11% discount and an overall 37% reduction from the original $135 price. Google then cut the number of shares it was selling from 25.7 million to 19.7 million — a 23% cut. In other words, the company reduced the supply. Fewer shares were available, and at a significantly lower price.

Well, when something is that unreasonably cheap and scarce, people should take notice. It's the same for shoes, clothes or concert tickets: When there's a limited amount of something and it's available at a discount, demand goes up.

The same happened for Google: Skeptical buyers eventually came in and bid the stock up by nearly 100% by the end of the year. As people began to realize that Google was a game-changer of a company, demand kept soaring. And since shares were no longer available at $85, investors had to keep bidding up the price until a shareholder was willing to sell. Obviously, you wanted to be the person owning Google shares at $85. That way you benefited when the price of its stock soared. That's the magic of understanding supply and demand — the basis of a stock's GoingUpness.

You might be thinking: Why haven't I heard about GoingUpness before? The reason you haven't heard of this strategy for analyzing stocks is because Wall Street doesn't want you to know about it. This is how the insiders make money, after all. If you learned about GoingUpness, you'd be invading their turf.

Wall Street elites will tell you this is all nonsense. Next, they'll smile and kindly tell you to leave your money with them instead. Then they'll suck their fees out of your investment cash without missing a beat. If the stock goes up, they'll take credit and tell you they are geniuses. Of course, if the stock goes down, they'll give you hundreds of reasons why they're not to blame. (They'll keep their fees no matter what.)

How do I know? As you may remember, my background is from Wall Street. I managed billions of dollars. So, you're not getting secondhand stories when you read my writing — you're getting information from someone who's worked on Wall Street and knows its secrets firsthand.

The sad, simple truth is that the people who manage your money on Wall Street don't care if you make money. They care about the cash they make: fees, commissions and bonuses.

Now compare that to my goal. I'm essentially invested in your success because your success is my success. Your failure is my failure. Our interests are perfectly aligned because, if you do well, you'll stick with me. Not only that, but I understand what you're looking for and how to get it. Like any investor, you want to make money in a timely fashion. You want GoingUpness, and my system is designed to bring you that. With it, I'll help you pinpoint stocks that have a good shot of going up soon, and for big gains.

I've spent thousands of hours researching how to get the best out of the stock market. And with my unique professional experience as a Wall Street insider, combined with my lessons from countless trial-and-error trades in which I tested this system with my own money, I've created something that works.

Of course, there are no guarantees in the stock market, so we won't pick up a winner every single time. That's simply the nature of the beast. When you invest, the future is uncertain. No system is perfect, and my GoingUpness system is no exception.

But more often than not, I expect to find winners instead of losers. And we can bag gains that most other investors will never see in opportunities they won't hear about until it's too late.

Inside the "GoingUpness" System

When you boil it down, GoingUpness is a simple system that looks to find cues to tell you if a stock will rise. As I researched and tested this system, I found that there are six main cues. It's possible to find a stock that has all six cues, but just keep in mind that it is exceedingly rare. Events like Google and Netflix just don't happen every day. If we waited for those, we could end up waiting years in between opportunities, all while perfectly good trades pass us by.

So, most of the time, we're looking for stocks with at least a couple of cues. And the most cues we'll likely ever see is four — and that's fine. In the end, more cues don't necessarily mean a better opportunity. In fact, depending on the stock, one cue can be more important than the rest combined. Think of it as if you're a detective. One great clue can solve the case. In another case, you might need three small clues to solve it. That's why I like to say that successful investing is not an exact science. Ultimately, it's an art — one in which you connect possibilities and make inferences between observations.

The key is not in connecting the dots, but in finding the right dots. With that said, let's turn to our six cues of GoingUpness.

They are broken up into two sets. I'll list them out and then give you the details of each one.

Set One:

The first set is comprised of the qualities you look for in a stock, and each quality ends in "ness." They are:

- InDemandness
- Insiderness
- Buyness

Set Two:

The second set are the three abilities that a stock needs to have. Each factor ends in "ability." They are:

- ScarceAbility
- ValueAbility
- ManageAbility

InDemandness

Now for the details. Let's start with the first set: "InDemandness" means that a stock is in demand among buyers. A company's tech can show InDemandness — rising sales, market disruption, a much-needed product or service — which will then grow the company and shoot up the share price. Essentially, InDemandness indicates investors will keep buying the stock at current prices or higher.

My GoingUpness system has two ways to measure, monitor and track this. Most of the time, an in-demand stock trades at or above its trend line. The 10-day moving average is the best example of the short-term trend line. Keep in mind that "trend" is just short for supply and demand. A dip, for example, means too many shares are being sold in the market, and that there's no demand for those shares at current prices.

A dip is not good if you own the stock. It means that supply is too much for the current demand. As a result, the current price of the stock can plummet. Most of the time, once it falls below the trend line, you can expect it to keep dropping. Because of this, we want to buy stocks that are at or above their trend lines. That is, stocks above their 10-day moving averages.

Secondly, we want stocks that are at least 20% above their 52-week lows. We use those numbers because an official bull run for a stock is one where a stock has gone up by 20%. And the 52-week low is an important indicator for investment analysts because if a stock hits it, it's probably headed lower. On the other hand, if a stock hits a 52-week low and then climbs 20%, it's officially in a new bull run, which is what we're looking to benefit from. Once a stock is in a bull run, we'll want to see it rise steadily to its 52-week high, because then it's a good bet that it will keep going higher.

Now, there are special cases in which this doesn't signal a solid stock. Stocks with very low prices can jump around by

20% or more in a single day. So, you have to use your common sense and judgment with this element of InDemandness.

In the end, you can see that a stock has InDemandness when it goes up two days in a row, with rising volume. In other words, more people are willing to pay higher prices for the stock one day later. When you see this happening three days out of five, for two or three weeks, that's a sign the stock is going to keep climbing.

Insiderness

"Insiderness" means that one of two things has happened to the stock recently that reveals insider knowledge.

One, insiders — namely the company's management — bought shares in the last six months, or they granted options to themselves. It's a good sign in particular if management buys back stock after a rapid decline. It means that they don't believe whatever put pressure on the stock is going to be permanent. It's also a sign that they think the stock is cheap and likely to go up soon.

Secondly, if you see one company buying another during a down cycle in the industry, or when stocks are in a bear market, that's another sign of Insiderness. Good management knows its business, so it can tell when the industry is bottoming out and when stocks are cheap.

Buyness

"Buyness" means that a stock is hard to buy. When a stock is being accumulated by insiders, they try to make the stock unattractive to other investors. An example is if the gap between the ask price (the price you want to pay to buy the stock) and the bid price (the price at which someone is willing to sell you the stock) is wider than normal. The difference, or spread, is typically between two cents and five cents at a maximum. So, in my picks, I look for a difference of 10 or 20 cents. A wide gap between the bid and ask prices makes the stock unattractive to naive buyers who don't understand what's going on. This tells me the stock is probably being accumulated by insiders who really don't want outsiders involved.

You may also find that when you go to buy the stock, the price keeps jumping higher or your order never gets filled — more deterrents. Another sign is sharp up-and-down spiking in the stock within the same day, which tends to scare people into selling their shares.

So, those are the three "ness" qualities that you want to see in a stock that has GoingUpness.

Now, let's move on to the three "abilities" that a stock needs to showcase its GoingUpness. As you might have noticed, I'm using different terms when describing the second set. These are "abilities" instead of "qualities." The difference between a quality and an ability is that an ability relates to the company's stock, rather than the people associated with it.

ScarceAbility

Now shifting to the second set, let's consider "ScarceAbility." This means there's a limited quantity of the stock so it is scarce, which is exactly what we want. Companies that constantly issue shares, especially ones that have just had IPOs (initial public offerings), are making their stock less scarce and, therefore, less valuable.

For example, many companies use shares to pay compensation and bonuses to their employees, and these can run into the millions. The technical term for this is *dilution*, and most investors don't track this watering down of the shares. Yet so-called "diluted" shares hit investors hard. It's like invisible selling, a tap that's dripping water all the time. And you'll mainly feel it when a bear market hits or investors panic for some reason — because that's when these diluted stocks crash.

We want to avoid these companies. It's actually fairly easy to do so, since ScarceAbility is simple enough to track. You just look at the shares outstanding that a company reports every quarter. It's that easy. By tracking this number, you can see if a stock is getting watered down from quarter to quarter.

Now, there's one more element to ScarceAbility that you need to track: share buybacks. This adds to a stock's scarceness, but you have to figure out the reason. Context tells us a lot in this instance. For example, a company may buy back shares to offset the watering down of its stock from compensation and bonus plans. In this case, that's not improving a stock's ScarceAbility — it's just evening out the playing field. And now many companies have a policy to that extent.

On the other hand, some companies are opportunistic. They realize their shares are trading at extreme discounts, so they go in and buy shares. That kind of stock buyback is what we look for.

Finally, large investor holdings can also make a stock scarce. For example, Warren Buffett has held more than 9% of Coca-Cola for 29 years now. Buffett's gains are so large, and the dividends he collects are so big, that he's likely to never sell a single share. That means 400 million shares of Coca-Cola are unavailable. So, anyone who wants to build a big holding will be forced to bid up the price to get their shares. Bottom line: Buffett's large holding of Coca-Cola makes it scarcer, giving the stock ScarceAbility.

ValueAbility

"ValueAbility" means that a stock has to control something of value, and there are two main types: One is that it owns a growing business, one where sales are rising, profits are expanding and free cash flow is soaring. That's the best kind of ValueAbility. That's because most people buy stocks for growth. So as growth becomes more reliable — for example, we continue to see sales rise in the company's quarterly earnings reports — a stock rises in ValueAbility. More investors are going to want it.

The second is when a company owns a highly valuable asset, such as prime real estate, a big stake in another company, a huge amount of gold or silver, a collection of valuable art, etc. Sometimes, the value could be the company's cash holdings. The key to this kind of ValueAbility, though, is that the stock must be selling at a large discount (20% or more) to the value of these assets.

ManageAbility

"ManageAbility" means that a stock's primary business is easily managed. Essentially, this means there's nothing innately wrong with the economics of the company. We should feel that it could be managed by an ordinary person and still do well. To quote Buffett: "When a management with a reputation for brilliance tackles a business with a reputation for bad economics, it is the reputation of the business that remains intact."

That's been my experience as well. A bad business won't become a better business because of brilliant new management. A bad business is just that — a bad business. And a brilliant new manager won't make a difference. Sooner or later, the business's internal problems are going to rise to the surface.

One way to gauge if a business is solid and easily managed is by looking at the language used in company reports or press releases. In my experience, companies that use jargon and technical language are often looking to hide things, such as a sales miss. Straight-talkers, on the other hand, put me at ease. If they can easily explain themselves, there's probably nothing that they're trying to hide.

As a side note, "ease of understanding" should also go for your trading decisions: You should only buy into stocks where you fully understand the risks and the opportunities.

So, if you don't understand the investment thesis for a stock, that's OK. Just pass on it. Wait for an opportunity that makes sense to you. That way, you'll always feel in control of your investment and your emotions in regard to the stock. Because, in the end, that's the key to being a successful investor: Don't get too low when you lose, and don't get too high when you win.

Navigate the Markets Like a Pro with These Easy Rules

I look at the stock market as a means to an end — a tool to financial comfort. And after spending decades as a professional and personal investor, I've developed a set of rules for how to safely navigate the market to ensure successful investing while fulfilling my goal of living a life of financial independence.

These are critical rules that go hand in hand with any area of investing — regardless of how much you invest or your personal goals for success. It's incredibly important that you read each of these rules before you start investing. And it's even more critical that you continue following these rules throughout your investing.

So please, make sure you read these. Print them out and tape them on your refrigerator or next to your computer. While I can guide you through these markets, ultimately, it's up to you to adhere to these basic rules for investing.

Basic Rules for Investing	
Rule 1	Never make an all-in bet.
Rule 2	Equal-weight all of the positions in our portfolio.
Rule 3	Build your positions over time.
Rule 4	Take profits on the way up.
Rule 5	Keep cash on the side.

Rule No. 1: Never make an all-in bet.

No one has a crystal ball to predict which stocks will go up the most, nor can anyone predict which stocks won't live up to their potential. That's why you never want to put all your money in one stock. Remember, volatility of one stock is always higher than the volatility of a diversified portfolio with multiple stocks.

Because of that, I urge you to own at least five of my recommended stocks in your portfolio. If you can, make it 10. That way, should any single stock go down due to the natural price fluctuations of the market, you're less likely to be affected because your winners will outweigh any possible losses.

At the same time, if just one of those stocks skyrockets, you profit.

You want to spread your money around and give yourself many opportunities to win. The best way to do this is to follow my next step.

Rule No. 2: Equal-weight all of the positions in our portfolio.

This rule is two-fold. First off, equal-weighting your positions means you should invest the same amount of money in each stock in our portfolio. You never want to put more money into one stock over the others because if that stock goes down, you'll lose a ton of money on that one position. By equal-weighting your portfolio, you give yourself equal exposure to the stocks that will go up the most.

To explain why, let me tell you a quick story.

When my kids were younger, I once took them to a pizza place. When the pizza came, I asked my kids how hungry they were. If they were hungry, I told them I'd cut their pizza into 12 slices, so they could have more than one. However, if they weren't that hungry, I would only cut it into four slices and they could eat just one.

Of course, what my kids didn't pay attention to is that it was the same pizza. Cutting into 12 slices versus four wouldn't make it bigger.

It's pretty simple concept, and my kids are too smart for me to play that game with them now. But it is the same with stocks.

You can have one share of Tesla or three shares of Square Inc. — both are equally good investments and are largely worth the same amount of money. Having more shares in one company doesn't make it a better investment in any way.

The second part of this rule is also pretty simple: Set a specific amount of money you want to invest in a stock — not the NUMBER of shares — and stick to it. Then, use that set amount as a marker for all of your positions across your portfolio.

Rule No. 3: Build your positions over time.

When a certain stock gets a lot of coverage in newsletters or in the media, it can bid up demand for that stock and increase its price. This is why, oftentimes, you'll see stock prices higher than your comfortable buy price. Be prepared for this.

One solution is to build your position over a few days, weeks or months — depending on your marker for how much you plan to invest. So, when you're ready to buy, you can simply invest a small amount of money in the stock, wait for the stock to "bottom out" or settle itself over time and then buy more shares.

Timing your buys is a key factor for successful investing.

When the market opens, the big institutions are the ones that make the most trades. These big money buyers can significantly bid up the prices, which could negatively affect your returns if you buy at the higher price.

To offset this, we want to come in when the small institutions are buying. This usually happens between 11 a.m. and 3 p.m., and that is the time when I suggest buying into your positions.

To that end, never buy more shares than you set for your equal-weight marker in Rule No. 2.

Rule No. 4: Take profits on the way up.

We can never be certain that we are seeing the biggest gain a stock will experience. Similarly, we can't be certain if those gains are temporary or will hold for a while.

Because of that, you want to take advantage and profit when you can. News reports, politics, mergers and acquisitions, earnings updates and many other things can affect great companies and bring down the gains. No stock ever goes up in a straight line.

It's important to take some profits when a stock's way up without selling your entire position. That way, you're able to shield yourself from the market's volatility while using the market as a means to an end.

Identify what matters to you — a down payment on a house, a family vacation, a new car, private school or your kid's college tuition — and sell 10%, 20% or even 30% of a position and put these gains toward the things that make you happy.

It's OK to sell just a small percentage of your shares until it's time to sell your entire position at the market.

Rule No. 5: Keep cash on the side.

Emotions are investors' Kryptonite. They are the No. 1 reason you don't get the gains you want and deserve.

Keeping some cash on the side serves as your emotional security blanket at times when the market is especially volatile. When you have what I like to call a "cash buffer," it brings comfort to know that you still have funds not tied to the market. It will help you get through the bad periods and reach the big gains.

More specifically, it makes you less eager to sell out of your positions during those short-term dips in the market, which are usually the moments when you want to be the "strong hands" and stay in. That way, you profit BIG when the "weak hands" who sold their positions rush in and bid the stock back up.

For most people, keeping at least 10% of what they can invest is what works best. If you want, you can have a little more.

Volatility is both a normal and sometimes necessary function of the market. And following these rules of the investing game is one way to guarantee safe and smart investing no matter the market climate.

Determining the Right Time to Buy

Everyone wants big gains. But there's something people tend to forget when they are searching for the next Google or Netflix. It's what I told you was one of the first things I did when I became a portfolio manager at Bankers Trust. I'm talking about diversification. It's critically important to diversify your portfolio so that you get the highest return possible and still get a shot at some of those high flyers.

For me, diversification means simply giving yourself many chances to win. The best way to do so is to make sure that no single investment you're in can make you poor, but every single one can make you rich.

When it comes to diversifying your investment portfolio, I sometimes use collectibles, just to go beyond purely financial investments. I collect antique gadgets — telephones, cameras, typewriters, gramophones and radios from the early 1900s. That's a good strategy for a number of reasons.

When it comes to stocks, you can get instant diversification by buying an index fund such as the SPDR S&P 500 ETF (exchange-traded fund). That's an OK way to diversify. But there's a smarter way to diversify that I bet you've never heard of. The great thing about this way of diversifying is that you get the safety of being diversified and you get a huge increase in returns. For example, in the current bull market, you'd have made 82% more in a decade just by using this way of diversifying.

You see, when you buy an index fund, you're diversifying through a basket of stocks. For example, the "regular" S&P 500 is a basket of 500 of the largest companies trading in U.S. stock markets. Here's the key thing for you to understand: The S&P 500 is cap-weighted. Cap weighting means that you end up owning more of the biggest companies within the basket.

In the S&P 500, Apple has a market value or "market cap" of around $607 billion. So Apple will have a larger effect on the S&P 500's movement than toymaker Mattel, with its $11 billion market cap. By market cap, Apple has a higher weighting — 3.5% of the index compared to Mattel's 0.02% at time of writing.

Turns out, there is a smarter way to diversify the basket of stocks in an index by equal weighting (rule no. 2). It's been proven smarter because the index goes up more. Way more. And it's not riskier.

Equal-weighted means that every stock in the fund has the same weight in the index. Big stocks and smaller stocks are treated equally. In a bull market, most stocks are going up. So, an equal-weighted index goes up more than the market-cap-weighted version because, in many cases, smaller stocks will make sharper, faster moves higher than larger stocks.

Don't get me wrong. You definitely want big stocks in your portfolio. But you want newer, fast-growing stocks that can zoom up too. If you use smart diversifying tools such as an equal-weighted index fund, you get the best of both worlds — the safety of big stocks and the growth of newer, smaller companies all in one.

Bottom line: If you're going to own stocks, be smart in your diversification of positions. The way to do that is to buy an exchange-traded fund (ETF) that uses equal weighting rather than cap weighting.

How to Deal With "Market Maker" Manipulation

The financial industry today is an incredibly dangerous place for those without experience. It may not be full of muggers in ski masks waiting around street corners to snatch your wallet, but there are "market makers" — some big traders employed by banks who run Wall Street — engaged in tactics that amount to the same thing.

Many people who navigate the industry by themselves don't come out unscathed. I know this because I worked on Wall Street for decades. I've seen the inner sanctum of the financial industry — and I'll say it again … it's not pretty. That's why I tell my readers to be cautious when dealing with these folks. In the end, they just want your money… and they don't have many qualms about how they get it.

A prime example is what happened during the 2008 financial crisis. Corrupt bankers and the crooked Wall Streeters nearly destroyed the economy to line their pockets. Sadly, nothing has truly changed.

We saw that laid out in vivid fashion most recently when these same folks used the Brexit crisis to manipulate stocks. After a shock vote in Britain to exit the European Union, a lot of unseasoned investors panicked. Now there was no reason to sell, and as we now know, the process of actually leaving would take months to years.

Using the cover of the theoretically oncoming Brexit, market makers slammed solid stocks in order to scare nervous investors. They sold companies left and right, forcing ordinary people to panic and sell, too.

After slamming stocks down for two days and getting people to dump their shares at cheap prices, the market makers bought them up at bargain-basement costs. Then, as investors came back into the market, those stock prices zoomed. We've seen it time and time again. It's simply their way to get money:

Skittish investors feel pressured to sell good stocks at dirt-cheap prices because of a temporary or fabricated panic. Then, when they eventually try to buy them back after the panic eases, they have to pay through the nose.

It's the classic Wall Street "slamma jamma" routine: Slam them down, jam them up again. This is just one of many routines they use to con people out of their money.

That's why I routinely say you can't trust Wall Street or the banks. They rig the markets to manufacture dirty profits from your hard-earned dollars. Ask anyone who's worked there. They'll tell you it's fixed, which is why many of them don't even have investment exposure to the stock market. It's truly a den of thieves, so it's crucial to learn ways to navigate that world safely.

You won't hear about this from the mainstream talking heads who show up on news channels because most of these folks are in on the game. Some even make plenty of its money from Wall Street advertising dollars.

That's why I've made it my business to give people the chance to make real money with real opportunities. I like to give my readers the inside scoop and warn them when a stock opportunity is too good to be true — and reeks of Wall Street scheming.

How You Should Sell: Limit Orders vs. Market Orders

When you go to sell, there are two types or orders you can set. The first, a limit order, means you specify a price that you want to get as a minimum. The second, a market order, means you take the price that is there the moment that you enter the order.

The type of order you choose depends on the kind of stock you own. Let's say, your stock is thinly traded or illiquid. In other words, it's small or not well known. Then, you'll want to use a limit order. In other words, you would set the price at which you want to sell. That's because often, the next price down from the order you enter could be 15% lower. You'll expose yourself to very low prices and get taken advantage of by the market makers. So, for thinly traded, illiquid, unknown or small stocks, use limit orders.

However, if you're dealing with a stock that is very liquid and trades hundreds of thousands or millions of shares a day — say, a very large brand-name company such as Coca-Cola or IBM — you're better off going with a market order. That's because you'll get the price that you see when you enter your order, or close to it.

The third thing you want to think about is why you're selling a particular stock. Is it because a piece of news has come out that has negatively impacted the stock or the industry it's in? Or did you think a company would keep growing but it no longer is? Did you buy a stock because you believed a company might get approval for something but that's no longer true? These can all be good reasons to sell your stock immediately. In all likelihood, there's going to be a long line of sellers who will follow your lead and who will sell their shares over the next few hours, days, weeks and even months.

You might also sell your stock simply because you feel you own too much of a single company and you want to raise some cash. If so, you can take your time and pick a day when the market is up to sell your stock slowly, in pieces, the same way you bought it. You might be selling based on your personal situation. I've used stocks to fund a down payment on a house and for a vacation.

I don't mess around when I sell a stock. I focus on trying to get my money out of the market. You should do your selling sooner rather than later if you simply feel you want to raise some money. It helps, of course, to keep a little bit more cash on hand so you can take your time and sell when it's most advantageous to you.

Why Stocks Can, and Should, Be Volatile

Of course, not all stocks move up or down in price at the same rate or by the same margins. My years of investing in biotech stocks have taught me one thing: Volatility does not equal bad. It's simply the nature of the beast.

You have to develop a strong stomach for volatility, particularly if you're going to invest in smaller stocks such as the ones you find in medicine and biotech. There will be a lot of news coming out surrounding these companies, and not all of it easily understood. A breakthrough drug might push up a single stock by 20%, 30% or more in a day. Then, at some later date, it might be revealed that the drug wasn't as successful as clinicians hoped or that it might not even get reviewed by the Food and Drug Administration (FDA) for months or years. New studies might show the drug to be a dud or even harmful, or that some alternative non-drug treatment is better. All of this is normal in biotech stocks. This is exactly what happened when I was working on Wall Street and scientists announced that they had sequenced the human genome that set biotech stocks soaring.

Typically, the more innovative a company is, the more volatile its stock price. It just comes with the territory.

Now that you know the basic rules of the game, here are a few more things you should know before jumping into the stock market:

7 Things to Know Before You Start Trading

1. If you haven't already, you need to open a brokerage account.

You need a brokerage account to buy a stock. Commonly used brokerages are E-Trade, Fidelity and TD Ameritrade — but there are many more. Some brokerages, such as Robinhood, let you trade for free using their smartphone app. Others, such as Tradier, let you trade at very low commissions. There's one called Stockpile that allows you to trade fractional shares — meaning you can invest $100 into a stock like Amazon instead of the minimum $1,700 for a single share.

I don't recommend using any particular brokerage. Choose one that has cheap commissions and whose website or app is easy and convenient to use.

2. The best times to buy stocks are during regular hours.

The best time to buy any stock is during the stock market's regular hours: between 9:30 a.m. and 4 p.m., Monday through Friday.

Within this time window, the best period for small investors to buy stocks is often between 11 a.m. and 3 p.m. That's because big-money investors tend to put in their orders at 9:30 a.m., and then around 4 p.m.

When big-money investors crowd into these times, they tend to drive stock prices higher. By waiting until 11 a.m., you're not competing with them to buy your stock — and often you'll get lower prices.

The worst time to buy any stock is during afterhours trading. This is between 4 p.m. and 8 p.m., when there are few transactions. Since there's just one or two sellers during this period, they're going to give you a horrible price, so steer clear of this time. Take it from my 25 years of investing.

3. Start small and build from there.

Stock markets can swing around like crazy from day to day. So you have to learn to use this volatility to your advantage.

Most investors buy their entire stock position in one day. However, in my experience, you should buy your stock in small portions. Yes, I'm aware you'll pay more in commissions for this. Still, you'll find yourself feeling more in control when you buy your shares in small amounts and scale up to the position you want.

For example, let's say you're buying 1,000 shares of a stock. Start with an initial position of 200 or 300 shares. Then add another 200 or 300 at a time at a later date, until your position is full.

One more thing: You're going to want to stop buying when your stock starts going up — but you'll have to fight this feeling.

Thing is, rising prices are a sign of rising demand, which means there's not enough supply of the stock in the market. That's good news. So even if your stock is rising you can still buy; simply fill your position to the amount you want and are comfortable with, even when the stock has gone up after you've bought your first slug of shares.

4. How much should you buy?

The biggest mistake you can make in investing is picking one recommendation and betting everything you have on that ONE company.

I urge you not to "bet the house" on a single stock. That's an easy way to lose your money in one fell swoop. Instead, you should diversify and own a series of different holdings in your portfolio to limit your exposure to any one company. Since this has been a problem in the past, I've come up with an easy-to-follow system, essentially based on common sense.

I recommend owning at least eight to 10 stocks in your portfolio, equal-weighted. For example, let's say you have $1,000 in your trading account. If you use my approach and buy 10 equal-weighted stocks, you would invest about $100 per stock.

With this approach, you have some padding so if one stock goes down, you're not crushed by only having invested in that one.

But I believe the stocks I select each have potential for hundreds or even thousands of percent gains within just a few years. And in my experience, just a few big winners will more than compensate for losses. That's why it pays to invest in several — you have more chances of hitting the life-changing winners.

I also recommend diversification between bigger, more stable new-world companies and smaller growth new-world companies. That way you get the safety of big stocks and the growth of newer, smaller companies all in one.

5. How to manage your losses.

While our goal is always to make money, you're not going to bat 1,000. No one does. Not even Warren Buffett.

So, at some point, one of the stocks you buy is going to go down. Stock markets can swing wildly from day to day, and in the last nine years, we've had three flash crashes where stocks fell 10% in a few minutes. We've also had two mini bear markets. And there have been weeks when the whole financial world looked on the verge of collapse.

Since we can't make money if we keep taking big losses, I recommend a 30% stop-loss strategy for most stocks. A stop-loss is essentially an automatic trade order given by an investor to their brokerage. Stop-loss orders can guarantee execution, but not price.

Here and there, if there are special conditions that warrant it, we may push this higher or lower. I even recommend suspending a stop-loss strategy when experiencing temporary market volatility. After all, it's perfectly natural for the market to have down periods, and some of these price movements are actually manufactured by the market makers who want to collect shares from you cheaply.

You don't want to sell out of good stocks that could pick back up again in a week or two, so sometimes it makes sense to hold on to your positions and wait through those down periods.

It's important to use closing prices to calculate your stop-losses because intraday prices can swing wildly. Flash crashes can happen in a few minutes, and then prices recover. So intraday prices are unreliable as a gauge of the true price of the stock on a given day. However, closing prices are real and backed by volume.

To follow this strategy, you have to commit to being OK with rebuying the stock. Many people have a problem doing this because they think the stock has lost its luster. But just remember that we're in this to make money — and that I'm working off 25 years of experience. Sometimes, the best stock to buy is one we've already sold.

So understand that if a stock regains its GoingUpness, it's okay to get back in — even if you were previously stopped out.

Investors who track their portfolios every day can use more advanced strategies to manage their losses. My strategy is to sell a stock when it drops below its 10-day moving average. If you want a longer time frame, you can sell if the stock drops below its 50-day moving average.

In the end, this strategy will save you money when a stock doesn't have GoingUpness anymore. In fact, this is why the elites on Wall Street disapprove of it. They say you can't time the markets that way. You should just know that this is, to be blunt, BS. They need you invested to make their fees, commissions and bonuses, so they never want you to sell. But sometimes, selling is simply the right path.

6. How to manage your profits.

Let's say your stocks have skyrocketed. You're ready for more gains, but you don't want to lose out on any future upside.

While many people believe that they should hold on to their stocks forever and milk them for every last penny, that's not the best idea for a growing portfolio.

My No. 1 rule in gains management is this: If you're losing sleep over your gains, sell until you stop worrying.

From time to time, it'll benefit you to take profits on some of our stocks.

Let's say a stock you own surges, and you want to buy into a new recommendation. However, you don't have the extra money. No problem!

Here's what you can do.

Sell some of your position when a stock becomes bigger than 25% of your portfolio. Then, put your gains to work in a new stock.

Now, this is a great strategy to use at first if you only own a few stocks, and you'll be able to use your profits to buy newer, growing recommendations.

The goal is to own all of your stocks in equal amounts. That way, you benefit from every stock that goes up. Plus, no single stock will ruin your portfolio if a trade doesn't go your way.

If you're a beginning investor, start with five stocks ... then buy into 10 stocks ... until you own a basket of stocks. Then, you can take profits evenly across the board whenever you want to raise cash.

If you need to use some of the capital that's tied up in your portfolio, all you have to do is sell a small slice of each stock. That way, you can still benefit if these stocks go up more. You don't want to miss out on a stock that starts to soar.

7. Finally, use your stocks to live a little better than you would without them.

So many people believe they need to hold their stocks forever. Personally, I think when you make money in stocks, you should enjoy your win.

This is something my father — and a lot of Wall Street suits I worked with — never really did. But I make it a point to.

Stocks are a means to an end. Enjoy your time and use your gains on family, friends, adventures or even toys. You can't really know why Tesla is so amazing until you drive one! Your time is more valuable than any stock.

With my GoingUpness system, in addition to my rules of the game, you'll get the chance at the big gains Wall Street doesn't want you to know about — and the chance to make your life a little better.

I promise you it's never too late to get rich or to improve your life through the stock market.

PART
-4-

**Building Your Financial
Future With the Big
Profits Unlimited
Mega Trends**

The stocks that have massive upside all participate in mega trends. These have significant influences on the financial markets over a longer term. While I am continually studying upcoming trends, today, there are seven that I feel are critical sectors to pay attention to as investors. I expect these stocks to go up for many years to come, creating the biggest bull market we've ever seen.

Mega Trend No. 1: The Internet of Things (IoT)

My father wasn't the savviest when it came to using computers. While kids and grandkids today are introduced to technology at birth, my dad didn't even have a computer until later in life. So it was something he never was too comfortable using. Despite this seeming aversion to technology, he still implemented computerized billing, collections and accounting at the company where he served as chief financial officer. To top it off, when I was 15, he made me take typing and programming classes.

The reason was clear to me: My father saw the future coming, and he knew it would center around computers. He might have not liked the technology, but he didn't fear it.

Instead, he figured out how to make it work for his business and his family. It's something I've taken to heart, particularly now, since we're on the cusp of the greatest tech revolution in modern history. This revolution offers the promise of incredible benefits and phenomenal financial rewards.

So now we all have the same decision to make as my father: We can fear the changes or, like my father, embrace and benefit from them. And there are a few great opportunities out there doing just that.

Now, the Internet of Things (IoT) is not something new. It's really been in development for a decade. If you look at it closely, as I have, you'll see that it's comprised of many different parts. One of those parts is sensors or chips, which are semiconductors that are measuring devices. These are things that monitor, track and accumulate data. The next step is that they communicate that data through a network. These are the wireless phone networks and broadband networks. Then, from there the data has to be stored. These are the data-server farms.

Once this data is stored, somebody has to make sense of all the information. That's done by the software companies. It's known as Big Data, the algorithms that over time morph into artificial intelligence (AI). So, these are the various different component parts of the IoT. The full picture of the Internet of Things has come about over time by seeing all these business-es come to exist separately — and then seeing the connections between very different things.

The tech revolution coming our way is driven by the Internet of Things. It's a tech revolution of smart machines that will reshape how we act in our daily lives — changing everything from the way we make breakfast (smart fridges) to taking our kids to school (driverless cars).

Simply put: It's going to infiltrate every facet of our lives. That's why the Internet of Things revolution is going to create massive winners in the stock market. And it's why those who choose not to capitalize on it are akin to the investors who didn't buy into the beginning of the internet and computer-net-working revolution of the mid-1990s. You may remember the types of profits traders saw back then. Early investors in Cisco Systems, for example, saw their stock go from the equivalent of about 14 cents in 1990 to $70 a share in 2000. That's an enormous gain of 49,900%.

These are astronomical gains that investors made simply from knowing how to be in the right place at the right time. And now there's a new "right place at the right time" scenario.

The market for Internet of Things IPOs has started heat-ing up. One key element of the IoT technological wave will be tiny devices called "micro-electronic mechanical systems," shorthanded to MEMS. For the Internet of Things to work, companies are going to put MEMS into everything — pipes, electric wires, doors, windows, locks, cars, airplane engines and medical devices. In short, you'll see it go into everything.

These miniscule devices — tiny as a pinhead — measure and transmit data. No more worrying about leaky pipes or short-circuited electric wires. Our cars will able to talk to each other and avoid accidents. Our ovens will be able to determine the right temperature and time to cook based on what we're baking. No more burnt cookies! These are just a few examples.

The industrial Internet of Things, where machines connect directly to servers and each other, is a subset of the larger Internet of Things. These devices will transmit data in real time that'll be stored on a server. All this collected data — Big Data — is hugely useful. I believe that in the next three to five years, virtually everything we make is going to be using Internet of Things technology — sensors, data collection, Big Data analysis — to run factories that manufacture everything from cars to cakes.

Let me tell you how this technology works. The first step in this technology is where sensors (essentially tiny micro-chips) are embedded into just about everything. These sensors are specialized for the particular environment in which they will work, as well as their purpose. These sensors are capable of tracking, measuring and monitoring data.

This data can represent a wide range of information, from temperature to usage levels, to weight or light readings. They can even track a heartbeat or movement. There are thousands of other categories of activity.

The second step is the transmission of these trillions upon trillions of data points. These data points are sent through wireless communication networks to distant computer storage systems, often referred to as cloud computing.

The third step is the analysis of this data, turning it into actionable information. Once stored, this data is analyzed to find trends and correlations, creating usable information. For example, the collected data might show how a machine operates when it heats up to a certain temperature. The machine operator can then use this information to determine the optimal way to run it so that production is maximized while potentially reducing energy usage, increasing safety or both.

Now imagine these steps being applied to more than just a factory machine but to health care, transportation, natural resources, food production and energy-efficient homes. Data-driven informational insights that increase efficiency and save money are the key to the IoT. The raw material underpinning it all is data. Each and every day we create the equivalent of four Eiffel Towers' worth of Blu-ray Discs filled with data. That's 2.5 quintillion bytes of data. An astounding 90% of all data that's ever been recorded has been created in the last two years — a clear sign that the IoT revolution is well under way.

Based on the thousands of hours of research and millions of dollars' worth of work I have put into this field, I can tell you that there is one single thing underlying the entire IoT field. This single component is critical: semiconductors, also called chips or sensors.

Semiconductors are the engines powering every element of the IoT mega trend: from robots, Big Data, artificial intelligence, self-driving cars and networked machines. The way I track the progress of the IoT is to check on shipments of semiconductors.

Just a few years ago, for instance, semiconductor shipments reached 900 billion. Now, that number is estimated to jump to 1 trillion shipments of semiconductors, according to research firm IC Insights. That's a huge growth.

Already, utility companies have begun to prepare for the Internet of Things economy. Many are putting sensors on lines at critical power junctions so that they have real-time data on the condition of this infrastructure. Companies are spending money to collect data on usage patterns to reduce costs. We will know exactly how much power is being used where and when. This is going to help us use electricity more efficiently and safely, and it'll cost less.

Here's a good real-world example to demonstrate the impact of the Internet of Things: At 4:10 p.m. on Thursday, August 14, 2003, the lights went out in New York. The hum of modern life, refrigerators, air conditioning, fans, computers, printers and office equipment was suddenly gone. The near-constant cacophony of traffic was silent. I was on Fifth Avenue in midtown Manhattan when it happened — the Great Blackout of 2003.

This was before smartphones, so no one knew what was going on. By 6 p.m., we learned by listening to battery-operated radios that the biggest power outage in U.S. history had occurred. An estimated 55 million people in seven U.S. states and Ontario Province in Canada were affected. No power meant no subway service. I walked seven miles back to my apartment in Brooklyn. People slept outside on the sidewalk because they could not walk up the stairs to their apartments 30 or 40 floors up.

I wondered what would happen in Brooklyn that night. I remembered the way people described the 1977 blackout. There were riots and looting through Brooklyn, with entire blocks set on fire not far from my apartment. This time, people left candles outside to help people see. Neighbors gave food to people with kids and helped the elderly into their homes. The New York Police Department reported less crime on that day than the same day the previous year with power. It was a shining moment from my time in New York.

However, the blackout of 2003 also showed how badly maintained and out of date our power infrastructure was. A congressional investigation showed that there were no common standards for maintenance and upkeep. Conditions for a blackout event of this scale had been building for some time.

Fast forward a decade, and the problem of infrastructure still exists.

Soon, I believe infrastructure spending is likely to go to power. This is a good thing because the biggest tech trend of the next 20 years — the Internet of Things — depends on reliable power.

Much of our current power and electricity infrastructure has its roots from the Electricity Act of 1926 and the Rural Electrification Act of 1936. Back then, we were transitioning to an industrial economy. Without government spending on the electrification of the country there was no way you could put up a factory in most small- or mid-sized cities and towns. Today, we're at a similar moment where it's absolutely critical for us to reorient our electric power infrastructure to the Internet of Things. This new technology is going to have machines that are monitored by people who are hundreds or even thousands of miles away. Think on the level of solving traffic issues, crime and even pollution.

A blackout similar to the one in 2003 would be disastrous in an Internet of Things economy. Blackouts mean big losses for most businesses that rely on computers and the internet to do everything, from inventory to billing to sending out money.

Already, electricity companies have begun to prepare themselves for the Internet of Things economy. Many are putting sensors on lines at critical power junctions so that they have real-time data on the condition of this infrastructure. Companies are spending money to collect data on usage patterns to reduce costs. Encouraging these efforts so that we know exactly how much power is being used where and at what time is going to help us use electricity more efficiently and safely, and it'll cost us less.

Companies also see the value of investing in the future of the Internet of Things. For example, Enlighted, a Silicon Valley energy technology company, claims its clients are saving as much as 60% to 70% on lighting and 20% or 30% on heating and air conditioning from this kind of infrastructure spending. Imagine scaling that up nationwide. Those are big savings, and it's one reason why I believe that companies that participate in infrastructure spending are going to do well.

Some of the smartest money in the world is already on the move in the IoT. In 2016, Japanese billionaire investor and visionary Masayoshi Son bought ARM Holdings, a computer-chip design firm, for $32 billion. This was a massive bet for Son, and the biggest one of his career so far. In fact, $32 billion represents almost 50% of SoftBank, the holding company (similar to Warren Buffett's Berkshire Hathaway) that Son founded. The cash deal also represented the largest investment ever from Asia into the United Kingdom.

At the heart of this big deal is the Internet of Things. ARM Holdings licenses its computer-chip designs for a fee. And the company is a free agent — it'll do the work for anyone who needs to put a chip into anything. ARM currently has its tech in smartphones, including Apple's iPhone. But the company is positioned to see its chips go into more and more devices, such as cars, sensors and household appliances. That's why the IoT is a mega trend I follow closely.

If you've heard of the IoT before, you may think it only relates to your personal technology, such as your smartphone, tablet or fitness tracker. But if you bought a new car in the last few years, chances are it too is an IoT on wheels.

Digital sensors built into the engine, tires and other compartments transmit data all the time. The onboard computer monitors wear and tear on the engine and transmission, and on the emissions, airbag, braking and stability-control systems. If there's a problem — maybe the tire pressure is a little low, or the oil filter needs changing — the system will let you know.

But that's just a small slice of the pie. The biggest potential gains are going to come from industrial machines.

For example, when you get on a plane today, the pilot's cockpit is, in essence, a computer-monitoring station, constantly measuring and comparing all the information pumped into it from the aircraft's myriad systems — engine, flaps, fuel system, landing gear and all the rest. Even a single jet engine is made of many different subsystems — fans, manifolds, valves and combustion chamber — each fitted with its own digital sensors for temperature, pressure and speed.

Virgin Atlantic, which has 17 advanced Boeing 787 Dreamliners in its fleet, is one airline embracing the Internet of Things. The carrier estimates that each of its planes generates half a terabyte of data (roughly the equivalent of 110 DVD movies) because every engine and airplane part is connected to a computer all the time. As a result, Virgin Atlantic runs a safer, more efficient airline with improved bottom-line results.

That's just one airline. Now, imagine the impact as every transportation fleet in the world. Every factory and assembly plant, and all their many industrial machines, are constantly connected to the internet. The operator of a metal-stamping press knows, before it happens, when one of his machine's parts is about to fail. He can anticipate maintenance, reduce downtime and improve efficiency. Same for the guy running a log-cutting machine at a lumber mill. He would know precisely when a blade or belt needs replacing and have the information to intervene before a terrible industrial accident occurs.

Collecting data, analyzing it and using it to increase performance, efficiency, safety and profits is the industrial IoT opportunity. This goes for machines that are in every factory or plant you see, whether they are making beer, cars or toys. The industrial IoT is going to be in every single manufacturing site where machines are being used to produce things. The company that controls the software operating system for the industrial IoT is going to end up being a mega growth company and a stock market blockbuster winner. Let me give you an example of how I found a great way to play the IoT mega trend.

Harness Cloud Computing's Limitless Profit Potential

The Internet of Things revolution is going to create massive winners in the stock market. And it's why those who choose not to capitalize on it will fall in line with the investors who didn't buy into the beginning of the internet and the comput-er-networking revolution of the mid-1990s.

There are astronomical gains that investors made simply from knowing how to be in the right place at the right time. And now there's a new "right place at the right time" scenario. It's something called "the cloud." I'm of course not talking about a physical cloud that floats in the sky, but the next stage of connectivity between devices made possible by cloud com-puting.

In its simplest form, cloud-based platforms are networks of various computer servers that all have a different function. Some servers might run a specific type of software, such as Adobe or Microsoft Office, while others can be used for data storage, such as Dropbox. Cloud platforms help businesses save money and increase their productivity because they don't have to store and maintain their own servers.

While this technology has made business operations easier in one respect, it comes with its own challenges. To put it sim-ply, cloud platforms require many different independent data centers to work together to keep networks running. That can be a nightmare for the people who manage them. The solution to this was the creation of something called hyperconvergence — or bringing all the different components of data centers to-gether into a single, scalable infrastructure.

Imagine having one server that could give you networking, computing and storage all in one device. The result is a system that both stores and processes data more efficiently, is more cost-effective and ultimately more secure.

One way I found to play this cloud IoT trend was with a company called Nutanix Inc. (Nasdaq: NTNX). I originally recommended this company in one of my newsletters, *True Momentum*. I'm not recommending this for you to buy, but to show you a great example of what I look for when I pick stocks. Nutanix is a cloud-based company that makes hyperconver-gence data centers that act as server, network, and storage all in one package. The company's goal is simple: to replace traditional IT products and data storage systems with its own Nutanix Enterprise Cloud technology. It allows anyone to access information stored from any device, at any location, and with limitless scaling capabilities.

The company saw some major success. Nutanix now has more than 10,610 clients in 145 countries and serves the world's leading companies, including Boeing, Toyota, McDonald's, AT&T and Sony, to name a few. A few years ago it had just under 1,800 clients.

Nutanix grew by developing a game-changing platform that's going to kick the Internet of Things into overdrive. Nutanix's software uses machine learning to analyze data it collects and stores for its clients. And as these machines "talk" to one another, they slowly start to learn and become more advanced.

This is a critical component of the Internet of Things revolution, which requires that different devices be able to send and receive data to one another. Based on my research, Nutanix has one of the only hyperconvergence platforms on the market and by far the most advanced. That's why powerhouse companies such as Google and IBM teamed up with Nutanix to build out their existing platforms and provide a more streamlined service to their customers.

I believe that as Nutanix continues to outpace its competition it will start siphoning money from older storage and cloud management developers. In fact, Nutanix estimates that as these older software makers fall by the wayside, it will stand to capture a combined $118 billion worth of revenue. Despite its massive market potential, Nutanix has a market cap of just $7.66 billion.

It was clear the market hadn't figured out the amazing opportunity Nutanix would bring to investors. Nutanix is in a niche market that not a lot of people knew about — yet. But as more people came to understand the artificial intelligence application of Nutanix software, big-money investors would come in and bid its stock price to the moon.

Nutanix's revenue skyrocketed from $241.4 million in 2015 to $1.16 billion in fiscal 2018. Analysts estimate that revenue will hit $1.94 billion by 2020. However, when I look at the enormous $118 billion revenue stream that Nutanix expects to capture, I believe that these estimates are far too conservative.

Analysts always give lowball numbers over fear of a company not meeting its expectations, so it was no surprise to me that they were not pricing in this stock's enormous potential. Even if Nutanix performed at the growth rate analysts were projecting, its stock was going higher. In fact, there was only one risk that went along with buying Nutanix. If the company issued more shares, that could dilute its stock price.

Yet because Nutanix's revenue was expected to grow at 36% per year over the following three years — which again was based on the conservative estimates of market makers — I knew its growth should easily outpace any share dilution we might run into.

Bottom line: Nutanix was a fast-growing company that will continue to benefit from the Internet of Things expansion, especially as more companies move toward hyperconvergence platforms.

Mega Trend No. 2: Robotics and Artificial Intelligence

My young son and daughter love when I tell them about new tech. And they're not shy about pinning me down for information about when they're going to experience the new technologies that I tell them about.

The one that most interests them is the one that many grown-ups fear — robots. Adults see robots as a growing threat that will steal our jobs. I can see where some would get that idea. Robots backed with AI are already popping up in different sectors.

Take Pepper — Pepper is the most sophisticated robot ever made. She can read emotions, do interviews, connect to cloud-computer systems and even express "feelings" in 20 different languages, all thanks to her unique programming. Pepper works at a bank. She greets and interacts with the customers.

You'll also find robot workers in hospitals, assembly line factories, airports, retail and even at fast-food chain Burger King. A new study forecasts that over the next 10 years, advancements in technology, automation, smart machines and globalization will touch nearly every job. In some cases, that does mean existing jobs will disappear, but so many more will be created. It's the future of jobs. Maybe one day my kids will want one of these jobs of the future and tell me they want to be an AI educator, a drone experience designer or a virtual-reality assisted surgeon.

And by investing in the future of the market rather than playing it safe, you have a much brighter future filled with gains than those who stay tethered to the past.

Companies in the U.S. and Canada are ordering a record-setting number of robots year after year. Projections from Boston Consulting Group show no slowdown in the spending on robots by industry. Companies are expected to grow spending to $24 billion annually by 2025.

I believe the robotics revolution will generate massive stock market winners, just like Microsoft and Intel benefited from the PC business, Google from internet search and Apple from mobile computing. Robots will become even more important as spending on this technology ramps up over the next 10 years.

Growth in robotics isn't just taking place in North America. It's a global phenomenon and massive growth is still ahead. As this progression occurs, the stocks of companies that make robots are going to rocket even higher than where they are today.

Just imagine going into a hardware store and, instead of having to hunt down an overworked employee — someone not only trying to guide customers but who's also stocking inventory, keeping an eye on customers and dealing with anything that goes wrong — you interact with a robot whose sole purpose is customer service. Imagine going up to this robot at your own local store and asking it for a hammer. It could then either tell you where this hammer is in the store, or if you prefer, it could take you there itself because it's mobile. You could take in a specific screw or bolt you're looking for and have the robot scan it and then tell you if the store has it in stock and where it is.

This robot would have a giant iPad-like display on its face that would allow you to use the robot like a computer. You could search the store for the thing you're looking for, or look up outside sources to help you figure out what you need for your project or work assignment.

Sounds like pie in the sky, doesn't it? It's not, though. This very robot exists, and if you were to go to certain Orchard Supply Hardware stores in the United States, you'll find a robotic clerk just like the one I described to you. I first came across the OSHbot when I attended the RoboBusiness Conference in San Jose, California, back in 2015. Since that time, the OSHbot has been renamed and is now called the LoweBot. The "Lowe" in LoweBot represents Lowe's, the home improvement store, which bought out the bulk of Orchard Supply Hardware's assets and locations and now treats the company as a subsidiary. Most people don't know this, but Lowe's has been investing in technology for three years now through its Lowe's Innovation Labs. It looks to use disruptive new technologies — such as robots, 3D printing and holograms — to give Lowe's new ways to keep its retailing experience competitive.

Another major investment trend I follow is artificial intelligence facial recognition. This technology can now spot a criminal suspect in a crowd of 60,000. It has already happened in China. A person was identified in a crowd of 60,000 people in a stadium and was implicated in a crime. Artificial intelligence plucked this person out of the mass of faces, which is really quite extraordinary when you think about it. How long would it take a human being or even a team of human beings to do that? Facial recognition technology is pattern recognition, which is artificial intelligence at its simplest.

Now, some of you will be horrified by the application of artificial intelligence in this particular case. However, just imagine if we had artificial intelligence at work on 9/11, scanning faces at the airport as the terrorists tried to board the planes. The attack might never have happened had we been able to identify people ahead of time using artificial intelligence technology.

It's a chilling example, I know. But I can tell you that most of the applications for artificial intelligence are quite simple and harmless, such as helping you find a better vacation and music, and advertising deals on products you have actually shown an interest in buying. AI is looking at your preferences and putting things in front of you in order to limit the amount of time you spend searching for what you want.

The reality is that artificial intelligence is changing every business model from the ground up. If businesses onboard right away, in all likelihood they're going to get left behind. AI is already used in any number of industries and it's moving really fast. AI should generate $3.9 trillion by 2022. McKinsey, another blue-chip consultant, estimates that, in time, AI will generate $3.5 trillion and as much as $5.8 trillion across 19 industries. Travel, transportation, retail, automotive and high-tech — these are the top-five industries that will be impacted.

Rise of the Robots: Tap This Disruptive Technology for Big Gains

Without even trying, new-world technologies are steadily becoming part of our daily lives. I'm talking about technologies such as wearable devices that monitor your heart rate, artificial intelligence that helps cars parallel park or household robots that map and clean our floors. So many new inventions are being discovered, developed and deployed at lightning speed. It's almost impossible to keep up. But there's one I've been watching for some time now that's disrupting the old world industries. I recommended it in two of my newsletters, *Profits Unlimited* and *Rebound Profit Trader*. I think it paints a great picture of a stock with true GoingUpness. Take a look at what I saw in this opportunity.

Teradyne (Nasdaq: TER) is close to a $10 billion company that has two main business segments. There's "regular" Teradyne, which makes test equipment for computer chips, circuits and complex electronic systems — all the component technology that goes into everything from smartphones to server systems and large industrial machines. Teradyne equipment helps companies become more efficient and improves the quality of their manufacturing.

But the company's biggest growth, now and in coming years, is set to come from its Universal Robots division, a pioneer in the field of "collaborative robotics" (or "co-bots" for short). Unlike traditional industrial robots — usually fenced off inside restricted areas of factory floors to prevent workplace accidents — collaborative robots are designed to work side by side, safely and efficiently, with a human counterpart.

It's a revolutionary concept. Think of a factory floor where a human operator oversees a precision milling machine. His one-armed robotic partner does the tedious part, stacking raw metal blanks. If conditions change, the robot can be quickly moved and set up in another area of the shop — stacking products on a wooden pallet, for instance.

Their general-purpose design and small size open up the use of co-bots to thousands upon thousands of medium- and small-sized businesses around the world.

Annual sales at Universal Robots have already increased an average of 75% a year since 2012, when I first recommended the stock. Revenue for the division had more than tripled since

2013, and profits before taxes more than doubled in the previous two years. At the time we bought in, my GoingUpness system indicated that big-money portfolio managers were getting ready to buy Teradyne's stock in droves.

That was great for us; these big-money portfolio managers were going to bid the stock higher as they built their positions up to their maximum point. Analysts would have to change their tune as well. They're often afraid to pencil in bigger numbers for cyclical companies like Teradyne, which typically see a trough in the business cycle for five to seven years, then much stronger business conditions for an equal length of time.

I expected Teradyne's business to surge higher, led by a global surge in spending for its robotics systems as well as for its core testing-equipment division. From experience, I can tell you that most estimates are too low. I expect growth of 10% to 15% per year as the spending wave on IoT sensors and devices ramps up its testing business.

Universal Robots was financially sound with over $1.1 billion in cash on its balance sheet. And in the last few years, it had generated over $1 billion in free cash flow. Free cash flow is the gold standard for knowing when a company is doing well financially, and Teradyne is a top-notch company by this standard.

Mega Trend No. 3: Precision Medicine

Thanks to the IoT, every device used on heart patients will connect to the internet. Pacemakers, defibrillators, stents, valves — everything will be connected. We'll take smart pills and get implants and all kinds of improvements in testing and tracking of diseases. But it goes even deeper than that with precision medicine.

I was born in a small town in India. My sister and I were the first kids in my family to be born in a clinic supervised by a doctor. My mother and all her brothers and sisters were born at home with the help of a midwife, or someone in the family who took the role of a midwife.

The thing is, despite this upgrade in where I was born, something went horribly wrong. The delivering nurse or doctor didn't sterilize the knife used to cut the umbilical cord. And a few days after my mother took me home, I got a nasty, spreading skin infection. For days, my mother went from doctor to doctor hoping that someone knew how to stop it.

Doctors in India at the time, especially in small villages, didn't seriously consider the critical role of cleanliness and sterilization in care. Days passed. The infection kept spreading. Finally, a doctor at the birth clinic guessed right, that this was an infection caused from birth and gave me an antibiotic.

Luck. Intuition. Skill. Who knows what made this doctor guess what it was because clearly it was something that was unseen at the time. We in the United States think of our health care and medical system as being a highly scientific process. However, in reality, the essence of the system that I experienced at birth — one that's based a great degree on a mix of luck, intuition and skill — is what we still have today.

Certainly, the kind of health care we enjoy in the United States is a massive improvement over what used to be. A Google search will show you that we did some horrific things to people back then — pedicle grafts, iron lung procedures, bloodletting, lobotomies, hysteria cures, poultices, nature cures and so on. Extremely unscientific stuff.

Yet today we are on the front edge of a revolution that's unfolding in health care and medicine. This revolution is being driven by being able to generate information on our medical conditions that we are now accumulating through electronic health records. Second, it's being driven by the rapid decline in the cost of sequencing our genetic codes.

These two things are going to allow us to take our information so that we can get a more precise diagnosis when something goes wrong. And then, we can be prescribed a treatment that maximizes our benefits and minimizes our side effects based on our specific genetic code. Precision medicine, I believe, is going to upend the current "unlucky schmuck" era of the health care system in the way that Amazon remade the retail business. It's a time of great risk if you're invested in the wrong companies. Equally, it's a time of incredible opportunity if you're invested in the right companies.

We will soon be able to get early warnings, whether it be of heart disease, cancer or any number of diseases. These early warnings are going to be generated through using information from our genetic code in combination with data in our electronic health records and data that is going to be collected from wearable devices. These new wearable devices are going to be able to measure and monitor things that will clue doctors in when you're on the way to a heart attack, or you're a candidate for cancer or some other devastating disease.

One firm I am researching, for instance, has already built the world's first medical "tricorder," to borrow a phrase from Star Trek. It's a handheld device like a smartphone that measures your body temperature, heart activity, pulse rate and rhythm, oxygen saturation, systolic blood pressure, physical activity and sleep. With this device, it takes your doctor only a second to figure out if you have a fever and should visit a clinic. Research shows that wearables are set to become a $51.6 billion market by 2021, with an annual growth rate of almost 16%. That's massive growth, and it's happening right now. This kind of device and the explosive growth that's coming are why I believe that the impact on our health and our health care is going to be transformative in a positive way.

This trend has actually been unfolding since we decoded the genome in the late 1990s. Our ability to understand what drives disease and change in the human body comes down to genes, enzymes and proteins. Before, we were using chemicals that had a probability of being able to change a disease; now we are able to start to make medicines that attack the actual disease itself.

Today, a medicine might fail to work for some while for others it might work really well. We don't know who it might work for and who it might not until *after* a patient takes it. Precision medicine gets us to medicine that is going to work for the individual based on his or her own genetic codes. We do that through collecting data and trying to match you to the exact medication that will work.

I strongly believe health care as it's currently practiced is close to obsolete. By obsolete, I mean that we're going to move to a new way of doing things. As an investor who's seeing this incredible transition happening, you want to get invested in the right stocks now, because the companies that are going to benefit from this new era in health care are going to skyrocket.

The new era of health care is going to be the era of precision medicine. Our current version of health care is incredibly primitive when you compare it to what we can now achieve using what we now understand about health. One of the main reasons we can now achieve superior outcomes is due to the fact that we now have incredible amounts of information about each aspect of our health, which are also now recorded in electronic health records.

These health records are data that can be parsed and sorted, then be used to make diagnoses that are based on information rather than an educated guess by your doctor. The difference is that a diagnosis based on your own actual health history is a significantly better guide to what is wrong with you. With computers, we can now use your personal records in combination with other people who are experiencing the same conditions, and we get an even fuller picture of what is causing the problem.

The second reason the new era of health care is going to be superior to our current version of health care is because of more effective drugs. The drugs we take right now are prescribed to us largely based on the selling ability of the company that makes the drug. In truth, most drugs only benefit a fraction of the people who take it — around 20%, just one person in five!

In effect, the era of Big Pharma is coming to an end. By Big Pharma, I'm talking about the dominance of companies such as Pfizer and Merck. Companies such as these created the modern pharma industry by coming up with one-size-fits-all drugs that doctors are persuaded to prescribe.

In truth, the real-world basis for prescribing the drugs that Big Pharma makes has always been suspect. Most drugs that meet the standards of clinical testing often fail in general use. That's because real-world conditions are nothing like the pristine, perfect conditions that you see in clinical tests. Second, and more importantly, these drugs simply don't work in most people because of small variations in our genetic codes.

Think about it: That's like making all clothing, hats or shoes the same size and design. For a small number of folks, those clothes may fit and appeal, but they don't work for everybody else.

Now, a new era of medicine and health care is dawning. And I believe that this new era is going to deliver better medicine that works in more people and through this, delivers better health care.

In the precision medicine model of health care that is unfolding, drugs will be matched to fit you. Instead of the pure selling power of a pharma company driving sales, you'll only get a drug if it has a high chance of working when you take it. And the way that's going to happen is through combining the information in your health records with genetic data based on your DNA, or your genome.

The bottom line of the new era of health care that's coming is this: Precision medicine is going to deliver the right treatment to the right patient at the right time. And the reason why it's going to happen now is because we spent an estimated $450 billion on prescription drugs in 2018, an increase of 9% over 2014. In general, the United States now spends about $3.3 trillion on health care each year.

By 2025, an astronomical $5.6 trillion will be spent on health care, according to the Centers for Medicaid & Medicare Services. We simply can't afford this. From my experience and research, I've found that innovations get adopted and implemented when the costs are too high and the benefits are so great that we feel compelled to dump the old and embrace the new.

Eighty percent of published drug studies are funded by the drug industry, which means that, in all likelihood, the drugs your doctor prescribes you have been sold to him by a representative from one of the big pharmaceutical companies. And you can be sure that these huge drug companies benefit big time from the random dumping of medications into those of us who get sick.

Now, don't get me wrong. Prescription drugs are a vast improvement over the bloodletting and witch-doctoring that was taking place 100 years ago, but I want more of a sure bet before I put some number of random medications into my body, or before I give them to my kids. Fortunately, that moment is fast approaching. New advances in molecular biology are getting us closer to matching people with therapies that will work more than a paltry 20% of the time. In fact, these latest advances have specifically helped to identify therapies for some of the most difficult-to-treat diseases, including different forms of cancer.

Embracing that mega trend will drive down costs across the board. The cost of decoding our genetic code is plummeting, down from $250,000 to $1,000 and even further — perhaps down to $100 soon. We are rapidly coming to a time when you will get a drug that is precisely suited for you, one that maximizes your medical benefits, minimizes your side effects and matches your particular set of symptoms.

Profit From the Precision Medicine Mega Trend

Now, let me tell you about a grand slam I found to profit from the precision medicine mega trend. Foundation Medicine (Nasdaq: FMI, now private) had all the makings of a mega-sized company. And just like all those companies, anyone prudent enough to have been there, on the ground floor (as we were), stood to make money hand over fist (as we did). I recommended FMI early on in my *Extreme Fortunes* newsletter. Then FMI was bought by Roche Pharmaceuticals.

Foundation Medicine is dedicated to transforming cancer care through the use of molecular information. This is the development of treatments informed by a deep understanding of the genomic changes that contribute to each patient's unique cancer. By offering a full suite of comprehensive genomic profiling assays, the company aims to identify the molecular alterations in a patient's cancer and match them with relevant targeted therapies, immunotherapies and clinical trials.

The goal is to improve day-to-day care for patients by serving the needs of clinicians, academic researchers and drug developers to help advance the science of molecular medicine in cancer. In short, Foundation Medicine was making big strides in precision medicine.

Why is this such a mega trend? Throughout history, medicine has been a one-size-fits-all enterprise. The medicine you take for a cold is the same medicine I take for a cold. But what if your cold medicine was specifically formulated for you, designed precisely for your genetic code?

Personally, I've never been much of a pill taker. However, 70% of Americans use at least one prescription drug. More than half take at least two. The most common drugs are opioids, antidepressants and antibiotics. In 2018, our total spending on prescription drugs was more than $360 billion. It rises steadily every year.

That number defines the opportunity in Foundation Medicine. For many people, taking a prescription drug is a cruel joke. When you look at most clinical trials designed to test a drug before it's approved, you'll find that the drug often only works in 30%, 40% or at most 50% of people.

For most people, most drugs won't work at all. That means at least half of our drug spending is junk science to make pharmaceutical companies rich. For some people, of course, the drugs do work as designed. For others, the drugs work a bit, though the side effects make using them a complicated decision. For many others, it's wasted time and money.

The fact is that most popular medications fail in around 40% of patients. Research shows that:

- Antidepressants fail to help 38% of patients.

- Asthma medicine fails to help 40% of patients.

- Diabetes medicine fails to help 43% of patients.

- Arthritis medicine fails to help 50% of patients.

And that's not over-the-counter medicine that I'm talking about. These are prescribed drugs, like the arthritis medicine Rituximab. It costs more than $11,000 for a two-dose treatment, and it fails half of the time. The problem boils down to the fact that each person has their own genetic makeup, and therefore needs a genetically designed prescription.

That's just the tip of the iceberg. The National Cancer Institute estimates that the number of people diagnosed with cancer annually will hit nearly 19 million by 2024. Few around the globe have been untouched by cancer, whether they're a survivor, or a friend or relative of someone who has suffered from the disease. CDC figures indicate at least one in three Americans who live to old age will be diagnosed with cancer in their lifetime.

In the United States, nearly $125 billion was spent on cancer care in 2010, and this number is forecast to reach $174 billion in the coming years. Meanwhile, more than half of the most common cancers can be traced back to specific genetic codes. That's why precision medicine is going to save millions of lives. We are already seeing doctors rallying behind this movement to engineer and prescribe medicine based specifically on one's genes.

According to the Personalized Medicine Coalition, 73% of new cancer treatments currently in early development stages will use genetic data in their creation. The MD Anderson Cancer Center — one of the world's most respected centers devoted exclusively to cancer patient care, research, education and prevention — performed a study on patients with end-stage diseases. It found that precision medicine increased the success rate by 440%.

Indiana University Health's precision genomics program did a similar study, and it had an 815% success increase for treating various cancers. Precision medicine represents the cusp of something truly revolutionary in the health care field. Foundation Medicine sits at the forefront of that development, set to be a disruptor of the health care industry.

Imagine if there were a way to figure out if a drug was going to work for you before you started taking it. You take a test, then you're matched up for a drug based on your genes. In other words, you're getting a drug that lines up with the way your body would actually use it, making it far more certain that the medicine will work.

That's the goal of precision medicine. It's an incredibly disruptive movement and technology with a goal to deliver medicine that's precisely right for your body. When this takes off, it's going to be a revolution.

Right now, we're flying blind. We're being asked to take pills based on a one-size-fits-all strategy. Just imagine if you went to a clothing store and found that they only sold one size — medium. The world would be filled with people wearing things that are too big or too small for them.

And that's where we are today with prescription medicines. Obviously, if you were a clothing manufacturer in this crazy world filled with people wearing the wrong-sized clothes and had the ability to make clothes in small, medium, large, extra-large and so on, you'd be sitting on a gold mine.

Well, Foundation Medicine is that manufacturer, and it is sitting on a gold mine. But you don't have to take my word for it. One of the world's leading pharmaceutical companies — one that's perhaps seeing the end of one-size-fits-all pharmaceuticals — bought into Foundation Medicine in a massive way.

Roche Pharmaceuticals is a Swiss mega-pharmaceutical company, the world's largest biotechnology company and the world's leading provider of cancer treatments. Twenty-five million patients annually are treated with one of its top-25-selling medicines. The company focuses on treatment in the areas of:

- Oncology.

- Neuroscience.

- Infectious diseases.

- Immunology.

- Hematology.

- Hemophilia.

- Ophthalmology.

- Respiratory disease.

Some of the company's most well-known pharmaceuticals include cancer treatment Avastin, osteoporosis drug Boniva, flu treatment Tamiflu and anti-anxiety drug Valium.

But Roche isn't limited to just its success in the development of effective treatments. The firm has been one of the world's most astute in its ability to anticipate the next big thing in the pharmaceutical world. It's perpetually ahead of the curve and ready to invest in this revolution.

For example, on February 2, 1990, Roche spent $492 million (about $937 million in today's money) to buy a 60% stake in biotech company Genentech. I was in college at the time of the purchase, but I still remember the press coverage. Wall Street analysts thought that Roche was crazy to spend that kind of money on an unproven technology. On tech that used drugs made up of things that already exist in our bodies, such as enzymes and proteins.

Despite the noise from Wall Street, the investment proved to be a grand slam for Roche. Genentech was not only a scientific and commercial success, but it also proved to be an enormous stock market success — a big enough success that Roche bought all of Genentech in 2009 for almost $47 billion.

Roche looked ahead and found its newest target for medical innovation — Foundation Medicine. The firm spent more than $1 billion to buy a 56% stake in Foundation Medicine. By 2018, it spent another $2.4 billion in a merger to buy the rest.

When I was a Wall Street analyst, I met with Roche's CEOs and I heard firsthand about their philosophy: When they have a deep conviction that a technology is going to be something that will revolutionize the world, they go big.

That's what Roche did with Genentech in 1990, and that's what it did later with Foundation Medicine. Roche spent $50 per share for the 15.6 million shares of FMI. It loved Foundation Medicine's technology so much, it had to buy a controlling majority stake — over 50% — to ensure that no one else could come in and snatch it. That meant Roche had to pay a huge premium to get that control, priced as if it were buying 100% of the company.

After the deal passed, Foundation Medicine's stock went back down to what it was before the deal happened. After, however, the stock steadily rose.

Knowing what would happen, I sent an alert to my subscribers after the initial Roche purchase. I told them to buy the dip, giving them a price that was 12% cheaper than what the Swiss drug giant paid. We were investing in the knowledge that one of the world's greatest pharmaceutical companies had checked out the technology and validated it with a $1 billion investment.

We also bought in while Foundation Medicine's technology and product set were better developed and established. Foundation Medicine's sales were $61 million at the time Roche made its deal. By the close of 2016, the company's sales came in at $116.9 million. In 2017, Foundation Medicine's sales were $152.9 million, well above company estimates. Talk about a growth stock.

One of the great things about Roche's investment in Foundation Medicine is that it de-risked Foundation Medicine for us. That's because the Roche deal gave Foundation Medicine more than $1 billion in cash. The company would not lack for capital to develop its technology, products and services. Because Foundation Medicine had enough capital, it wouldn't have to issue shares again to the public to raise money for these kinds of things. That's good if you owned Foundation Medicine stock because it meant that shares would remain scarce.

Also, the influx of Swiss cash removed any financial risk in the stock. In other words, there was no chance of Foundation Medicine going bankrupt. Roche validating the technology before investing meant that we were buying into a sure thing, at least as sure as anything that you're ever going to find on Wall Street.

Many investors likely would have preferred to wait until Foundation Medicine was more established. This is where part of my three-part system comes into play. My strategy is quite complicated, but to help explain it, I break it down into three phases. I'll quickly go over each of them.

The first phase is what I call disruption analysis. I determine if the company is an industry disruptor. To uncover this, I research a company to see if it's going to change the entire industry the way Netflix changed watching TV, the way Apple changed phones and the way Amazon changed shopping.

Finding disruptors is one of the foundational pillars for grabbing a multi-digit gain. This could be a new drug, a new technology, a new system for doing things or a new medical device. The list is endless. But it has to disrupt the industry. And — this is key — I pay close attention to the potential market size for this disruptive company. If the potential market is small, the stock can only climb so much. If it has a big potential market, the stock can easily climb much higher.

When it comes to Foundation Medicine, you could see that the company was set to disrupt the industry with the use of its precision-medicine approach. What's more, its approach was wide-reaching, stretching far beyond more effectively treating cancer patients, extending to a variety of illnesses and diseases.

The second phase is the number-crunching phase. Once I know a company is going to disrupt an industry, I need to make sure it has the potential to go up dramatically. I look at a lot of numbers. Some are really basic. For example, I look for companies with a market cap of $150 million to $2 billion. Sometimes I'll push this to $3 billion depending on the stock. That's because they still have a lot of room to go up.

There are dozens of other numbers I look at, but one of the most important is sales growth. I want to find companies that currently have under $3 billion in sales while growing sales an average of 10% to 20% a year. At this rate, a company would double its sales within five years, something that (without fail) catapults the stock price higher.

While Foundation Medicine's sales were above my usual range, we had the added bonus of Roche's purchase of shares. That helped to de-risk the stock, making it an incredibly attractive buy.

And, finally, the third phase of my strategy is insider activity. While most people look at what Wall Street is doing and what the media is saying, I just want to know what insiders are up to. After all, nobody understands a company the way a CEO or COO does.

Tracking insiders helps me get into a stock right before it's about to soar higher. A special kind of insider buying happens when insiders issue themselves stock options. And when you looked at Foundation Medicine, you saw insiders issuing themselves stock options hand over fist.

FMI insiders started doing their secret buying in April of 2016. They continued their purchases in June and October. In my experience, this is typical behavior by insiders. They tend to buy six to 12 months ahead of a stock rocketing higher. The reason we care is because insiders have the ultimate scoop on a company. They potentially know when sales are picking up or if a big contract is getting signed or renewed. The key concept is that it pays to follow what the insiders are buying. It's a giant heads-up to you that insiders believe the stock is soon going to rise.

And that's exactly what we saw with Foundation Medicine. The insiders loaded up, and they were expecting shares to keep rallying. That was our cue to get in on the stock and ride it higher as positive news of Foundation Medicine products got announced. To find great picks like this one, look for companies playing to the precision medicine mega trend and vet them using my GoingUpness system. Stick to the rules of the game, and you can ride your way to massive gains.

Mega Trend No. 4: Millennials

Back in 1929, the stock market crashed. For the next 10 years, the U.S. economy sank into a depression that put one out of every four Americans out of work. In 1939, World War II began. And in 1945, it ended. Those are 15 years of nonstop horrible events.

When World War II ended, everyone expected the Great Depression to continue. Many expected an even worse financial depression. But that's not what happened. Soldiers returned home. They married, got jobs and started businesses. They had kids and bought houses. Most importantly, they pushed aside the horror of war and depression from the previous 15 years. They set their goals to build a better life. And by doing this, they grew the U.S. economy by incredible amounts.

Between 1945 and 1955, U.S. household net worth nearly doubled, going from $728 to $1,429. The stock market boomed. The Dow Jones Industrial Average went up 133% from 1944 to 1955. Then the post-World War II economic boom just kept going. By 1965, U.S. household net worth was $2,531, nearly 250% higher than 1945. Stocks? The Dow soared another 150% between 1954 and 1964. We should take a simple lesson from this: Markets can boom when all recent events and persuasive analyses suggest pessimism and doom are a lock for the future.

The fact is the United States is facing a new generation that has the potential to move the market just as much as the boomers did. It's hard to top the problems the country faced in 1945. And yet one of the greatest stock bull markets of all time began in 1945. One of the key ingredients in creating the new market: a young, optimistic generation willing to make their world into a prosperous place.

And that's precisely what we have in the millennial generation. In fact, research shows that millennials are the most optimistic generation the United States has ever seen. Seventy percent believe they are going be better off than their parents, and 50% say the country's greatest years are ahead.

In the United States alone, the millennial generation is 92 million strong — making it the largest generation in U.S. history.

All of them have had technology — such as the internet, cellphones and smartphones — at their fingertips for their whole lives. They have witnessed the globalization of business and economic activity, where information and data are the critical factors.

A Bank of America Merrill Lynch study estimates that the global population of millennials is 2 billion strong. That's about one in three people on the planet!

In the United States, millennials represent 28% of the population, and these young people are going to be the richest generation in our country's history. Right now, millennials already account for $1.3 trillion in annual consumer spending. And that's set to grow. Research estimates that their yearly incomes will rise to $8.3 trillion by 2025. In addition, millennials are also going to inherit a record $40 trillion in assets from their parents.

The growing wealth potential of the millennial generation means that this group will drive buying trends, tech developments and more over the coming years, creating great investment opportunities if you know where to look.

This is why I so strongly recommend stocks in companies that explicitly target the massive growth in income and spending to be generated by the millennial generation. My research says that millennials' desire for experiences over things is driving their spending choices. That means millennials are more willing to spend money on travel, vacations, music festivals and outdoor activities. Travel companies such as Expedia and Priceline, for instance, could benefit from millennial spending.

You could see the same for outdoor-oriented companies such as Columbia Sportswear and Cabela's, which have trounced the S&P 500 Index over the past few years. The reason for this outperformance is the surge in spending by millennials on these activities. Millennials as a generation are poised to become a mega trend in the stock market. Their size, income and spending habits will generate massive stock market winners for you.

Companies that can help capture moments for millennials are looking at a massive opportunity. And there's one sector that is really benefiting from this "fear of missing out" (FOMO) trend. Every day, all day, millennials are plugged in.

For the millennial generation, posting their lives as they live it shows their friends, their family and themselves that they are not missing out. Their posts, pictures, tweets and Instagram photos prove it. For the companies who provide the services, all this activity is great — for selling advertising.

The essence of all these services is that users are generating content for free. Sure, it costs money to have big computers to save all this stuff, but that's just a drop in the bucket against the amount of advertising you can sell. And having people create content for free saves a lot of money when you compare it to old media companies, such as newspapers, which have to pay writers and editors to come up with content. That gets expensive.

It's one reason why these social media companies are so profitable. Facebook spends just 15 cents in direct cost for every $1 it generates in sales. In other words, it has a gross profit margin of 85%. That's insanely profitable! Even after counting indirect costs, such as research and development and administration, Facebook still has crazy-high profit margins of 35%.

Simply put, social media companies' costs are incredibly low because users create the content. That means if social media companies get millennials to use their services — which encompasses a lot of people — they can make massive amounts of money through advertising.

Facebook is only the beginning. Other social media stocks have as much or more potential. For example, there's Twitter, LinkedIn, TripAdvisor, Yelp and Match.com. In the future, you could see huge new stocks come to the market for social media, such as Nextdoor and OfferUp.

There's more big money to be made in the social media sector. That's because all of these companies are working off the same trend — getting millennials to put their experiences up as content and then selling advertising against it to make huge amounts of money.

For example, when Jim Cramer first coined the term FANG, everyone was looking forward to the massive potential of those exciting new stocks. Facebook, Amazon, Netflix and Google became must-haves in any successful portfolio.

Since that moment, I couldn't stop thinking about it. And finally, I came up with my own version of FANG that reflects our current society and millennial driven trends. I call it "STUF." The companies that make up STUF are advancing and changing the world right now. These all-star picks have the potential to surpass FANG. You may have guessed it by now, but STUF stands for Spotify, Tesla, Uber and Facebook. All four of these companies are taking the tech advancements of today and pushing them into the future.

Spotify (NYSE: SPOT) is the dominant music streaming service that I believe is used by every single person 40 or under, for the most part. CDs are gone. Regular radio is gone. Pretty much everyone uses Spotify. It truly captures the essence of how the millennial generation is spending its money listening to music.

The second is Tesla (Nasdaq: TSLA). Now, you might think that millennials don't have enough money to be buying Teslas. But I would tell you that is untrue. I know a lot of millennials who own the Tesla Model 3. They love Tesla. On top of that, most of them began their relationship with Tesla by buying a few shares of Tesla stock. Tesla represents technology, coolness and transportation for the millennial generation. There is a clear identification with the brand that is of our time.

The third one is Uber (NYSE: UBER). I remember the first time I used Uber. Guess who told me about it? A friend of mine who is a millennial. So, I tried it out — and I've never stopped. I've stopped renting cars and, at one point in time, I could see myself just using Uber all the time. Uber is now a publicly traded stock. Both Tesla and Uber have a strong grip on transportation innovation.

The very last one is Facebook (Nasdaq: FB). Facebook, of course, is used by everyone. However, Instagram, which is owned by Facebook, is what millennials use all the time to record what they are doing. Every time they are out doing something, this is what they use.

These millennial stocks are going up, and I believe they are going to continue going up. All four of these companies embrace technology. They not only make the world an easier and more accessible place, but they also have the brand recognition that's necessary to keep the general population's attention for decades to come. The same way that the famous FANG companies did, I believe the four companies that make up STUF have the same pull with the up-and-coming generations — if not more.

Change is truly the only constant that matters to serious investors. Take, for instance, the Internet of Things. Again, it is going to create a productivity revolution in everything that we do. At the same time, the U.S. millennial generation — the 92 million people born 1981 through 1996 — will start buying houses and cars as their incomes rise and they mature.

A key question to answer is what new technology, developments and other lifestyle expectations will the millennials want now and in the future? For example, big-box stores didn't exist until the baby boomers desired them. They essentially remade retail in their image. If you identified that trend early on, you made a lot of money on Home Depot stock, a 45,000% return! Same is true for streaming videos. Gen X influencers moved from renting VHS tapes and DVDs from Blockbuster to ordering videos from streaming super giants like Netflix. If you had invested $1,000 in Netflix in 2002, it would be worth around $326,000 today.

We know Blockbuster went bankrupt. And we are losing old department stores, too. Sears, Toys R Us and other brick-and-mortar retailers of the world are closing down, only to be replaced by online services like Amazon. And that's just retail. Imagine the impact on auto buying, banking, vacation, real estate and travel. It's endless.

I believe that the millennials will soon come to their own preferences on retail and buying. So, identifying those stocks that benefit from their spending preferences will be a way to play this trend.

There's been a lot of commentary about millennials living in their parents' basements and not making or investing any money. But, when you look at the facts, millennials are not only the most educated generation in history, but also the largest demographic in the workforce. Ultimately, they are going to replace the people who are in business today, and they're going to bring that education to bear. At the same time, they are also the ones who are going to benefit from the Internet of Things. Because of that technological shift, which is just by its very nature more profitable, millennial incomes are going to be significantly higher.

You use your income — and that stimulates the economy. Economists have written books about how this works and the patterns that take place when a generation comes of age. They call it "household formation." That's the economics term for when you tend to see growth on a home-building boom, and that's also when stock markets boom.

Mega Trend No. 5: Autonomous Vehicles

"Will I need to learn to drive?" my son asked me recently. Before I tell you how I answered him, I want to give you an idea of why he asked me this question. You see, right now, we're at a moment when things that once seemed permanent are now in question. Cars and driving are one of these things. There's been a sharp decline in young people even getting their driver's licenses. It's tumbled by nearly half since 1983.

Just to get a sense of car history, consider this: Nelson Jackson, Sewall Crocker and their dog Bud made the first successful transcontinental automobile trip in 1903. Car technology was primitive. They relied on stagecoaches to ferry spare parts. At one point, a cow had to tow them. Another time, a team of horses had to be sent to get them out of a Vermont bog. The 4,500-mile journey took 63 days, 12 hours and 30 minutes.

Few then would have imagined what happened next. Incredibly, the U.S. went from 800 cars in 1900 to 458,500 in 1910, to 8.2 million cars by 1920, to 276 million in 2017. That's an insane level of growth.

Car growth has exploded even higher in recent years. In 2018, U.S. vehicle sales totaled 17.5 million, not far from the modern record of 21.77 million back in 2001. However, I'm incredibly pessimistic about car sales because I believe that we've seen their peak. In 10 years, we'll have fewer cars on the road. And fewer still in 20 years. So what was my answer to my son? I told him it's unlikely he'd need to learn how to drive.

The reason I'm so pessimistic is because new innovations are going to wipe out cars as we know them. The average price of a car is $35,000, but the costs of traditional car ownership go far beyond the price tag. There is also interest paid on car loans, insurance, taxes, fuel and maintenance. Some expenses are not so obvious, such as parking, property taxes and construction costs for home garages, and the value of our time. And according to research by the Bureau of Transportation Statistics, our cars are only used for about 4% of the day.

In other words, buying a car is one of the most wasteful expenses imaginable. If you take that 4% number at face value, it means a total wipeout for the auto industry. It means we could get by with 96% fewer cars if we had a system that uses the cars we own. This same study also says that, right now, as many as 25% of people are better off using ride-sharing services, such as Uber and Lyft, that you can call from your smartphone.

I believe this study is right. The automobile of today is the equivalent of the horse-and-buggy transportation system of the 1800s. It's primed to be replaced by a new transportation system that's fueled by electric, self-driving, internet-connected cars — a system that will completely change transportation and, in time, life as we know it. Waymo, the autonomous car unit of Google parent Alphabet, already has plans to start testing this new kind of transportation system. Driverless cars could also be completely redesigned, such as to include a dining area.

There is also the ability to access vehicles rather than owning them, where you can choose from an entire fleet of vehicle options tailored to each trip you want to make, according to Waymo CEO John Krafcik. People could claim the cars for a day, a week or even longer, he said. We've already seen this option with Zipcar.

Now, you may think that this forecast is too strong. You may believe that because cars have endured for as long as they have, people will continue to rely on them. Yet I think cars as we know them are doomed. That's because self-driving cars have gone from a sci-fi-like idea to something that we're seeing on streets today.

Ride-share company Uber — one of my STUF companies — has already introduced a self-driving car in Pittsburgh. Uber's cars are Volvo XC90 SUVs, retrofitted with electronic components that make them self-driving. Now, it's still early in the development of this technology. Uber's cars are manned by a person who can take control of the vehicle when it hits a situation that it's not programmed for, or if there's an emergency. It's a bit like putting a plane on autopilot with a person at the controls just in case.

Yet Uber's self-driving initiative has 100 cars as taxis in the streets of Pittsburgh. If you use the Uber app, you could get a self-driving car sent to you the same way you do now when you place a ride request. Uber is looking to test the technology on passengers, pedestrians and other drivers in real-life, real-time conditions — and get data to adjust and improve everyone's experience with these cars.

Many people are skeptical about self-driving cars ever working out. They believe that it's a technological fad. And if it does work, it'll take 20 or 25 years to pan out. Personally, I believe that self-driving cars will become a usable reality in the next three to five years. For sure, it'll be a novelty at first, like many new technology experiences of the past. However, the convenience of being able to take a car to your destination without having to worry about traffic, routes, weather hazards, accidents, road rage, irritation, boredom or potential threats from a driver is a powerful factor that's going to make self-driving cars a massive hit.

By a massive hit, I mean that it'll take off and be something that people take to in the same way that people took to the iPhone and iPad. And clearly, the stock market agrees with me. That's why you're seeing stocks associated with self-driving cars shoot up by triple digits.

The keys to self-driving cars are sensors and data, and then computers to process this data. These things form the essence of a revolution that's taking place in the Internet of Things mega trend. And it's going to change the way we transport ourselves around the world.

Now let's think about the secondary effects of a self-driving car revolution. The highways you and I drive on each day came about because of a 1956 law, promoted by President Dwight D. Eisenhower, that built 47,856 miles of highway across America — the interstate highway system.

If our lawmakers approve more spending on roads and bridges, we're going to see billions of dollars go to companies that are involved in infrastructure. And the result of this spending is going to benefit companies that are shelling out billions to develop self-driving cars. I believe that quite a bit of the infrastructure spending on roads is going to actually make our roads ready for self-driving cars.

Beyond the actual roads, we also need standardized traffic lights. Self-driving cars would be easier to run if all traffic lights had a common design. That way, a self-driving car would only need to recognize one kind of traffic-light configuration. We could also better standardize road signs, road line markers and road lighting. By standardizing these things, it would reduce the complexity of conditions that a self-driving car would need to understand and make their introduction and operation smoother than under current conditions.

But regardless of what happens in Washington, we'll see money spent by the private sector to further the development of self-driving cars. That's because car companies are making big investments on this technology. Ford has doubled the staff on its self-driving initiative and is spending $150 million on a laser-based sensor that's a critical component for this technology. Mobileye, a maker of seeing technology for self-driving cars, and Delphi, an auto-parts maker, have agreed to team up to build their own laser-based sensor.

The critical point is that a huge wave of spending is coming to build out America's infrastructure. I believe a lot of that money will be used to build up our transportation system to accommodate the future of self-driving cars.

Mega Trend No. 6: Blockchain

There's almost nothing worse than waiting in line at the DMV. My last visit there to renew my driver's license was brutal. It didn't matter that I'd shown up right when the Department of Motor Vehicles (DMV) opened. I still ended up wasting most of the morning sitting around in a hard, plastic chair.

The experience itself was brutal, but not unique. Birth certificates, Social Security cards, passports — these personal identification records are a pain for everyone to get replaced or renewed. And the cost is our precious time. But what if there were a better, faster way to prove that you are who you say you are? One that could remove the old time-consuming method of paper identification?

Back in August of 2017, I said that I'd be willing to get "chipped" if it made my life easier. A lot of people thought I was crazy for even suggesting the idea of putting a chip in my body. But if it means that I could ditch my wallet, my license and my passport ... and never again waste time getting these items renewed ... I'm all for it.

We now have the capability to make this idea a reality with an invention called blockchain. It's basically an unalterable electronic record that can hold all of our personal information in one place. With a single chip connected to the blockchain, we could carry around everything we'd ever need. And it would reduce a lot of the bureaucracy we currently deal with in order to gain access to our personal information.

Many of you know the word "blockchain" because of virtual currencies such as bitcoin. However, the platform underpinning bitcoin and the vast number of so-called "altcoins" is this robust technology called blockchain. It provides a high level of security and is ideal for financial transactions. I'm looking especially close at companies and stocks that are looking to use blockchain.

If you've bought bitcoin, then you know that you can use the Square Cash App to buy it. That makes it easy to do. You move your money into the app, you buy the bitcoin, they tell you what the price is, you press "buy" and then you've bought it. After that, it starts to get a little bit different than, say, buying a stock. The biggest difference I noticed is that about six minutes after I bought my first piece of bitcoin, I got a text message that said my transaction had been recorded on the blockchain.

Now, that's a really mysterious thing because I didn't, at the time, really know what the blockchain was. I had some understanding of it, but once I saw that message it motivated me to do the proper research. I soon began to understand why this blockchain technology is so valuable.

Let's compare buying bitcoin to buying a stock. When you go to buy stock, you go to your broker's website and then you enter your order. The order is quickly confirmed. Now, you may not know this, but it actually takes three days before that transaction closes. The reason for that goes back 70 or 80 years. Back then, an investor would commit to buy a stock and sometimes renege. Then if the stock fell, they'd turn around and say: "Well, sure I'll buy now that the stock went down."

As a result of that gamesmanship, the markets developed a series of protocols that made sure that the person buying the shares had the cash and was good for the transaction. On the flip side, the person selling would also have to come through. Way back, that process would take over a month, sometimes even two months, to settle a simple stock transaction. Today, computers can do this work much faster. What stops stock trading from being faster still is the same thing that caused the problem to begin with: We still don't know if someone is good for the money, and we still don't know if the person who's selling the stock has the stock to sell.

That's where blockchain technology comes in. (Again, blockchain, not bitcoin.) Blockchain records all transactions from the beginning. Everything is recorded in a digital chain that can be instantaneously accessed, meaning that the person who needs to make sure that the buyer has money can be sure just by looking at the blockchain. The buyer can, in turn, be sure the person selling the stock is good for delivering it. The transaction closes fast, and you get a message similar to what I got when I bought my first bitcoin, which is that your transaction has been recorded on the blockchain.

In fact, anyone can see the transaction. It's public. It thus becomes very easy to see that the ownership of a given block of shares has changed.

The critical thing we need for blockchain to take off is faster computers and an infrastructure that allows for that data to build up in the blockchain. That way, it can all be accessed instantaneously. And that's happening.

Obviously, this has implications outside of just the stock market. Imagine a home sale, a process that takes in excess of a month, if you're lucky. Imagine the efficiency of the blockchain in shipping, supply chains, voting — the list is endless. I'm bullish on blockchain technology because I see so many applications where you can implement the technology and increase efficiency dramatically.

Just imagine if all your information could be contained in an electronic record that simply could not be changed unless you personally allowed it. And to allow a change, you would have to go through a secure chain of specific actions on your own. Now every time you went to apply for anything that requires an ID, whether it be a passport, a driver's license or a credit card, you could simply allow that company, organization or government officer to access your blockchain. It would quickly verify all your identity transactions, all your financial transactions or whatever was relevant. No more DMV!

People spend an insane amount of time standing in line — like five to eight years of their lives. We could wipe this entire process out and, in time, I believe you could even wipe out carrying an ID altogether.

No one I know likes chasing after their wallet, keys and driver's license daily. Or panicking because they left their passport at home. Equally, most people I know would love the benefits of going wallet-less, keyless, license-less and passport-less. Imagine being able to wave your hand and pay for things, or being able to start your car without a key. Imagine opening the door to get into your home without turning a knob, or being able to go through security and immigration without showing anything.

I'm aware of people's objections to chipping. However, our phones already collect huge amounts of data on us. Google knows everything you do online. Facebook knows everyone you know. Amazon knows everything you buy online. Visa and Mastercard know everything you buy. Radio-frequency identification (RFID) chips are already in things such as E-ZPass, I-PASS and SunPass — which let you go through toll booths. They are also in passports and some ID tags.

Getting chipped isn't going to change much in terms of our privacy. You could argue that by making the chip more personal, we'll become more aware of our data. We'll pay more attention to how much of it we share. Then we'll be more on guard because we're aware of being active generators of data. We'll insist on real restrictions on data collection and use. That's a better deal than what we have now. Google, Facebook, Apple and Visa all simply take our data by getting us to click on their 100-page user agreements. No one reads those. Even lawyers skip through them and click OK.

Right now, the fear of getting chipped makes it unlikely that most people will get one. However, remember that all successful innovations start small. There are always objections and difficulties. This was true for the train, the car, the computer and cellphones — even paper money. In the end, convenience, cost and a better way of life always win out. I believe that will be true for chipping, too.

In fact, it's a perfect marriage of two technologies: an embedded chip and your own blockchain. You would never need to carry ID because all of your information — data which today is largely recorded on scattered pieces of paper or in various electronic records sitting in computers around the world — would be contained in a chip on your person. You could carry around with you everything you'd ever need. You could walk straight through airport security and not even slow down to open a bag. The authorities would have cleared you as you walked down the concourse, drinking a coffee.

There are two big ways for you to get in on blockchain without even investing in bitcoin. The first way is to invest in cloud computing companies. The blockchain is going to require us to store lots and lots of information securely. Pretty much every piece of information that you currently have on paper is going to go onto a computer in a secure way that nobody can crack. So that's going to require computing power.

The second thing we'll need is very fast computer chips — and a lot of them. Semiconductor manufacturers that specialize in processing cryptocurrencies such as bitcoin are going to benefit from blockchain being expanded out from cryptocurrencies and moving into everyday uses. These include identification, finance, trade and so on. The future is in chips, and chips are most useful to us when they talk to the blockchain.

Lock in Big Gains From the Blockchain Revolution

In the future, everything you do, every bank transaction you make, every shipment you track and every record you keep will be recorded on a blockchain network.

This technology will replace the decades-old, backward-looking ways of the past. Think about it. Our economy is still practically stuck in the Stone Age, relying on paper contracts and proof-of-identity cards for everything — from getting a driver's license and voting to buying a house and traveling out of the country.

At best, these records are easy to lose track of, and at worst, they're easy to manipulate, leading to issues such as identity theft and loss of income. Some industries such as health care have moved their records online, but even those databases aren't safe from professional hackers.

The point is, our personal identities aren't anywhere near as safe as the government would like us to believe. But blockchain offers a solution. With it, we can change the way we store personal information and effect transactions for goods and services.

Blockchain will make life simpler and safer at the same time. Hence, the biggest companies in the world are scrambling to become early adopters of this new tech. In fact, my research shows that a combined $4.5 billion has already been put toward the adoption of this technology, with money flowing in from companies such as Google, Overstock, JPMorgan Chase, American Express, Reuters, Intel, Walmart, Nestle, Hitachi and Dole, to name a few.

IBM has publicly pledged to lead this technological revolution. Microsoft has launched a multimillion-dollar project to promote blockchain tech, stating: "We are seeing a lot of momentum and excitement in this space." And the CEO of Nasdaq called blockchain "the biggest opportunity we can think of over the next decade or so."

But it's not just tech companies that are taking notice. America's 10 largest banks have invested $267 million into companies behind this innovation. Last year, less than 15% of all banks used blockchain. Now, 80% of financial companies expect to adopt it within the next 24 months.

Add to that a recent study by IBM that revealed that 90% of all governments worldwide are moving to implement blockchain by the end of this year. And it doesn't stop there:

- The Centers for Disease Control and Prevention are planning to use blockchain to keep more accurate and easy-to-access medical data, potentially saving thousands of lives.

- Governments around the world are in the early stages of using blockchain to manage real estate titles. In fact, the state of Vermont recently authorized the first real estate transaction on a blockchain.

- Shipping companies are already using blockchain to manage their supply chains. Penske, FedEx and dozens of other companies have signed on to the Blockchain in Transport Alliance (BiTA).

- Small companies plan to go public and raise capital directly on a blockchain, eliminating the need for initial public offerings that require them to pay Wall Street's exorbitant fundraising costs.

- Even fundamental government functions such as voting and recording marriage licenses could be done on a blockchain network in just a few years.

Like I said before, the possibilities that blockchain offers are nearly limitless. But there is one catch — and it has to do with the computers that give us access to the blockchain network.

Every computer has the same basic parts, including a motherboard and a memory chip. And while these components are important, they pale in comparison to the part of your computer called the graphics processing unit (GPU).

GPUs use special programs that help them analyze and store data. This makes them perfect for performing certain tasks — one of which is figuring out complex mathematical and geometric calculations.

This makes GPUs perfectly suited for crypto mining and running blockchain applications. Because of this, the GPU industry has exploded as both companies and individual users alike have begun to integrate blockchain technology. Industry research shows that GPU growth is going to rocket higher over the next several years. Allied Market Research estimates that global GPU sales will bring in $157 billion by 2022, growing at a rate of 35% per year.

However, this figure is largely based off the growing crypto market because, currently, GPUs are mainly used to mine coins and make crypto transactions. However, as I just described, there are many more uses for blockchain that go far beyond cryptocurrencies.

And as more industries develop blockchain technologies, they'll need superpowerful computers to help run those applications. Right now, the entire blockchain industry has a net valuation of $4 billion. But it's expected to ramp up to a $3.1 trillion industry as new tech develops in the years ahead.

That's an incredible 77,400% rate of growth, and the kind of market opportunity that we want to take advantage of.

Remember, large organizations such as IBM all the way down to individual crypto miners are all competing with one another to get on the ground floor of the blockchain revolution. And that means they're all vying for the fastest GPUs on the market.

Right now, just two companies on the market make GPUs with anywhere near the computing power necessary to handle blockchain's complex algorithms at a competitive rate. And this makes them both incredibly valuable. While one of these companies is a well-known Wall Street darling, the other is a smaller, cutting-edge firm offering the same GPU capabilities at a more affordable price point.

Advanced Micro Devices Inc. (Nasdaq: AMD) is a global semiconductor device company based in Santa Clara, California. It specializes in manufacturing products for microprocessors, chipsets, graphics video and multimedia products.

While AMD is participating in several emerging technology markets, the segment I'm most interested in is its computing and graphics operations, which is the part of its business that builds GPUs for PC desktops and notebooks. AMD offers multiple tiers of GPUs for its clients to choose from, but arguably its most popular processor is its Radeon RX graphics card. This is appropriately comparable to Nvidia's GeForce GTX card, which is the company's main competitor.

While Nvidia traditionally beats AMD in terms of power for its higher-priced products, AMD makes up for this with its competitive pricing in its lower- and mid-range products. Typically, AMD GPUs are a couple hundred dollars cheaper than comparable models in Nvidia's line. And while this may not sound like much money in the long run, the savings add up when you consider how many chains of computers are required to solve just one block of data in a blockchain. For crypto miners building their own computer rigs at home, those savings can go a long way.

Better still is AMD's ability to turn a profit on the income it's generating. Now, one of the things that I always look for when making a new recommendation is future growth. One way to determine that is to look at the industry the company participates in to see if it's on the rise. Considering that the entire market for blockchain could soar by 77,400% or more, I'd say this industry is more than healthy!

The second thing I look at is the company's product. More specifically, I look at whether or not the product or service being offered is in line to grow with burgeoning market demand.

Looking at AMD's future net income projections, management is forecasting that future sales will quadruple income of just a few years ago. No one knows a business better than a company's own management team, so this gives me great confidence in the fact that we're buying into a healthy — and sustainable — business.

Considering the massive amount of data that computers linked to blockchain need to process, more server farms are being dedicated to crypto mining and other blockchain-related services. Aiming to suit the needs of these server farms is a new AMD product line called the Radeon Instinct Vega series, which adds to the company's growth prospects. These are chip-laden cards geared specifically toward the artificial intelligence and machine learning techniques used in today's server systems.

Analysts expect that this new series will show up in a variety of different workstations. The Vega series of chips will be twice as powerful as anything AMD has ever released, while still reducing how much electricity the system uses.

This efficiency is key to the future success of the Vega line-up. Faster, stronger chips cut down on the amount of energy needed to run through these algorithms. They're also cheaper and more efficient, meaning that hobbyists and professional miners alike are going to choose AMD products over more expensive options like Nvidia's.

Server farms consist of hundreds of server systems. AMD's products will allow miners and blockchain companies to save on the initial cost of buying the chips, as well as the power to keep the systems running. An increase in sales means more money will flow toward AMD's bottom line, which will cause its share price to rise. And that means more money in our pockets.

Consider that both the central and graphics processing units — and blockchain markets the company competes in — are set to soar. Even if AMD ends up capturing a small percentage of this market share, early investors are still going to see a sizable return on their investments. You could end up making five to 10 times more from your money on just this one stock alone, and that could add up to millions of dollars for those who want in.

It's important to get in early on trends like this before more companies and government bodies start adopting blockchain into their infrastructure. That way, as the industry grows and more computing power is needed, we get the benefit of AMD's stock soaring to new levels as people turn to its processor solutions. This example is great to keep in mind when finding ways to play a mega trend. It goes to show you that there are always ways to buy in even if it's not the obvious buy.

Mega Trend No. 7:
New Energy Technology

Traditionally, investing in energy used to mean putting your money into Big Oil. Not anymore. In today's world, next-generation energy sources are the best and brightest ways to pocket gains of 1,000% or more. Right now, the energy market is evolving quickly, with a focus on cleaner, safer and more efficient alternatives to old-world power sources such as oil, gas, coal and other fossil fuels.

In the next three to five years, we will see new applications of solar energy, hydropower, wind-driven turbines, fuel cells, electric vehicles (EV) and machines that don't run on fossil fuels. These are what I call "the new energy." It is sourced locally to the end user and is both storable and portable — meaning it can be generated in one place, stored and easily moved to another place for use.

All of these features of new energy have the potential to disrupt three huge existing industries: fossil fuel-based enterprises, utilities and transportation. The total stock market capitalization of these three industries is in excess of $7 trillion.

My research shows that new energy firms have the capability to dominate all three. Like Amazon did with retail back in the 1990s, and Netflix and Google did with media and information in the 2000s, these new energy firms will rise up to dominate how power is generated, sold and used. In the process, they are going to wipe out businesses that rely on old-world energy sources and industries tied to them.

Consumer demand for these new renewable and sustainable forms of energy is driving tech developments that will reshape the nation's power grid over the next three decades.

You can see it in the popularity of solar-power pilot programs in sun-drenched states such as California and Florida. It's clear from the growing number of electric vehicles — Teslas, Priuses and Nissan Leafs — sharing the road with you these days. And just look at car-charging stations popping up on American highways. These vehicles will not only cut down on environmental pollution and carbon emissions, they will also reduce energy costs. And, of course, they provide an incredible investment opportunity as the new-world energy sources rise up to replace old-world fossil fuels.

If you've traveled outside the U.S., as I do, you've seen these trends aren't only happening within our nation's borders. On a global level, fossil fuels accounted for two-thirds of the world's energy supplies in 2018, according to market research. By 2050, that will be down to one-third, while the remaining two-thirds will come from non-fossil fuels that emit zero carbon emissions.

Most of that renewable energy will come from wind, solar and hydro power. For wind and solar, it's a "50-by-50" prospect — meaning these renewable energy technologies will supply nearly 50% of world electricity by 2050 — ending the era of fossil fuel dominance in the power sector.

I see solar power making the most growth — rising from 2% of the world's electricity generation today to 22% in 2050, according to the research my team has assembled. A lot of that growth will come from behind-the-meter solar-powered cells in households and businesses, which will account for 5% of world electricity in 2050. Wind power is next in line, on track to generate 26% of the world's electricity in 2050, compared with just 5% today.

In addition, hydropower will experience only modest growth — in part because so few untapped sources remain. Meanwhile, nuclear power generation is not likely to grow by much, in part because of its high operation and waste-storage costs.

And, of course, with all the growth in renewable energy comes an investment opportunity. Just look at these numbers:

- Since the beginning of this year alone, over $117 billion has been invested into renewables by companies around the world, according to a recent Bloomberg analysis.

- That number is set to reach over $700 billion by the end of this year, new BBC research shows.

- And just one segment of the new energy market — the electric vehicle market — is projected to grow 715% by 2030.

All told, my research tells me that we will see $13.3 trillion invested in new power generation assets between now and 2050. Of this, 77% will go to renewables — wind ($5.3 trillion), solar ($4.2 trillion) — and another $843 billion will go to batteries. Investments in new fossil fuel plants will not exceed $2 trillion. This works out to around $416 billion per year.

As demand grows, so too does the grid, with distribution and transmission expansion needing an estimated $11.4 trillion by 2050. So, the U.S. electricity system will gradually phase out aging coal and nuclear plants with cheaper renewable energies (principally wind and solar) and gas, which will become the country's premier sources of power generation.

By 2050, most coal and nuclear plants will completely disappear from the energy mix, pushed out by age and economics. Globally, solar power is on track for a fourteenfold increase, and wind a sixfold increase over the next 30 years.

By 2032, there will be more wind and solar electricity in the world than coal-fired electricity. Gas-fired power will grow just 0.6% per year by 2050, supplying system backup and flexibility rather than bulk electricity in most markets.

Several other countries will also make huge shifts to renewable energy — including China, Brazil, Mexico, Japan, India, South Korea, Australia and most of Southeast Asia, the Middle East and North Africa.

Interestingly, all of this change will happen as global power demand grows by 62% between now and 2050, or by 1.5% per year. So what we're seeing is a revolution in energy that will rival — and trump — all of the industrial revolutions of the past. And we're just now standing on the brink.

Even now, more than two-thirds of the global population lives in countries where solar or wind, if not both, are the cheapest sources of electricity. Just five years ago, coal and gas dominated that picture. By 2030, new wind and solar will ultimately get even cheaper than running existing coal or gas plants almost everywhere.

That's because the average cost of solar and wind technology — and the power they generate — is falling dramatically and will continue to plummet in coming decades.

Of course, none of these advances will be possible without new battery technologies to store all of that new renewable energy over the next three decades. So, I see a battery revolution on the horizon as well. To help store excess energy from solar and wind to use when the sun isn't shining and the air is still, about 359 gigawatts of battery backup will be added to the power system over the next 30 years.

To visualize how much power that is, consider that a single gigawatt equals about 1 billion watts. That's enough to power about 110 million LED lights and would take more than 3 million photovoltaic (PV) solar panels to generate, according to the U.S. Department of Energy.

State-of-the-art electric vehicle charging stations and in-home plug-in systems — where vehicles batteries are powered up when idle — are already starting to play key roles here.

Battery prices are already down 84% since 2010. And market research shows the expansion of battery manufacturing for electric vehicles will continue to drive down the price of batteries.

Other advances in battery tech will make energy storage even cheaper and more efficient for wind, solar and other sources in the years ahead. By some estimates, battery costs will fall 64% between now and 2030.

Over the next five years, market researchers project more homeowners and businesses will add PV and battery storage systems. This will happen as companies and consumers alike recognize that such PV/battery systems may cost more upfront to install than conventional energy sources, but pay off over time. All told, my research shows that businesses and households will invest $1.9 trillion in PV/battery systems over the next 30 years.

There are also other amazing advances being made in battery storage capacity. That smartphone you have that needs to be recharged every day? New tech will allow you to charge it once a year or less.

And charging up your electric car overnight, which now gets you a few days of driving, will soon take just five minutes and allow you to drive for months — and thousands of miles — between charges. It's clear to me that we are transitioning from carbon energy to various new forms of energy. Some you are familiar with, such as solar and wind power. Others are emerging, such as lithium and hydrogen.

There's also a change in the way we're using this energy. We want our energy to be more portable, which means it's going to be smaller. And we want energy to be able to be stored, so this is going to change the way our energy infrastructure works. The last thing we're looking for is for energy to become more local. This is a massive change for energy infrastructure, which is a large part of our economy. I believe there are going to be big winners and big losers in the energy space. Winners here will generate thousands of percent in returns for investors who recognize these trends early.

New energy, as I define it, is energy sourced locally to the end user. This source could be the sun, wind, waves or geothermal heat. The other key aspects of new energy are that it is storable and portable. It can be generated in one place, stored and easily move to another place. All of these aspects of new energy have the potential to disrupt three huge existing industries — the legacy fossil fuel energy industry, the utility industry and the transportation industry.

The total stock market capitalization of these three industries is in excess of $7 trillion. My research shows that new energy firms out there have the capability to dominate all three industries. Like retail and Amazon back in the 1990s, and Netflix and Google in the 2000s, these new energy firms could go on to dominate how power is made, sold and used.

What's more, these new energy solutions are going to wipe out businesses that rely on the "old-world" energy and utilities industries. But it will provide an extraordinary opportunity for new companies to come in and make a fortune.

One chemical is crucial to this emerging investment opportunity: lithium. Now, alternative energy sources such as wind and solar aren't new. But they come with one major drawback: The wind doesn't blow at all hours of the day and the sun doesn't shine all the time. So either you use the energy as it's being generated or you lose it.

This becomes an obvious problem when you consider that people need 24/7 access to electricity. For a long time, new, so-called alternative energy sources were used as aids to existing power infrastructure. Now, thanks to battery storage technology, that's beginning to change.

According to a Navigant report, lithium-ion batteries have become the leading form of energy storage for all new energy projects. While there are many different factors that play into renewable energy storage, these core characteristics make lithium-ion batteries superior to their competitors:

- **Weight.** Lithium-ion batteries are about one-third the weight of lead-acid batteries. This makes it easier for maintenance technicians to swap them out once they can no longer hold a charge. It also makes them ideal to put into cars and other transportation vehicles.

- **Space.** Lithium-ion batteries are smaller and more compact, so they take up less space wherever they're installed.

- **Temperature.** Cold weather has much less of an effect on lithium-ion batteries than on lead-acid batteries, so they can be used in harsher climates.

- **Voltage.** Lithium-ion batteries maintain a higher voltage than lead-acid batteries as they discharge. This makes them ideal for solar use because you can run these batteries for a longer amount of time at their optimal voltage.

Lithium-ion battery systems are thus becoming attractive to new energy producers. But they aren't just a superior product. You can also get them at a much cheaper price point than even a few years ago (and the cost is projected to keep going down). That means lithium-ion battery usage will continue to gain momentum in the years ahead, especially as the EV trend starts to dominate the auto industry.

Considering that people are turning to low-maintenance EVs as a replacement for high-maintenance gasoline engines, it's only a matter of time before electric cars are the dominant vehicles on the road. As EV sales increase, the demand for lithium will rise. And the lithium market is already booming.

Right now, the No. 1 use for lithium is batteries — specifically, the kind of portable, rechargeable batteries you see in electronics and electric vehicles. But the off-grid energy storage market presents another unique opportunity.

An off-grid system is designed to work in remote locations outside of a normal electrical grid. It's beneficial to people who live in difficult-to-reach locations and for small communities that don't need a huge power supply. It can also be used to aid an existing power grid that is prone to blackouts or that doesn't run efficiently.

A great real-world example of this exists today in my garage. With this car, I can go from zero to 60 mph in just four seconds. And it doesn't make a sound. I can drive for over 300 miles without charging or paying for a single drop of gas. I'm talking about Tesla, the American electric car maker. It quickly developed the world's largest lithium-ion battery in Australia as a legitimate backup power supply. A powerful storm knocked out much of South Australia's power grid in 2016, and the country went into political upheaval over it. One part of the state wanted to rebuild its infrastructure with coal-fired power, while the other wanted to focus on renewable, green alternatives such as wind and solar power.

When Tesla CEO Elon Musk caught wind of the situation, he tweeted that Tesla could fix the energy capacity problem within 100 days or he would complete the project for free. His proposal was to build a battery storage grid that could provide between 100 megawatt-hours and 300 megawatt-hours of energy. That's enough juice to power 300,000 homes for an hour if the state experiences a blackout. Australia accepted Musk's bet, and he made good on his promise. Tesla completed the project in 60 days and turned on the power grid in late 2017.

But this is just the beginning. You see, the thing that makes Tesla's batteries so powerful is that they're scalable. Tesla recently developed a home-scale energy system called a Powerwall, which can provide power to your home and requires next to no maintenance to run. It's used in tandem with Tesla's solar panels, which you can monitor with the company's cloud-based software. The sun charges the battery during the day, then it drains overnight to run your home. A Powerwall and solar panels can save a family living in a four-bedroom house thousands of dollars in energy costs.

Off-grid energy solutions have the highest potential to take off in countries with unreliable power, such as India. Since lithium-ion batteries get cheaper to make every year, new energy companies will be more likely to use them in their power grids. Combine this with the fact that battery storage facilities offer people cleaner, more reliable energy, and lithium-backed energy solutions have the potential to disrupt the entire utilities sector.

Today's leading energy companies — Exxon Mobil, Royal Dutch Shell and Chevron — represent the old world. If they don't adapt, new energy companies will come in and obliterate their businesses. That creates a potential $780 billion in combined market value open to a willing competitor. Now, that's not to say these titans of industry are going to disappear overnight. But as new energy companies move to the forefront and begin to provide people with better energy alternatives, I believe these old-world companies are going to go extinct.

Spotting the Energy Company Fueling a 700% Gain

When renowned inventor Nikola Tesla designed the first alternating-current (AC) electricity system some 133 years ago, little did he know the extent to which his breakthrough would revolutionize the world — not once, but twice.

The first time was in the late 19th century, when Tesla's experiments led to the lightbulb. He also discovered the rotating magnetic field, which is the basis of most AC machinery. It also pioneered such breakthroughs as X-ray imaging, generators and wireless communications. In fact, his 1891 invention, the Tesla coil, is still used in radio technology today.

Fast forward to now. The use of electricity has become a crucial part of our daily lives. It powers everything from our homes and factories to our personal devices. It is so prevalent that we've come to take it for granted. We assume it will always be there for us no matter how great the demand. But the critical role of this potent power source in modern technology is about to make a major comeback. The catalyst will be a big event that will usher in a new era of electrical innovation.

You see, up until 2007, electricity usage in the United States had constantly increased. In fact, since the time that electricity was first used in the late 1800s until the 2000s, we produced and used more energy almost every year.

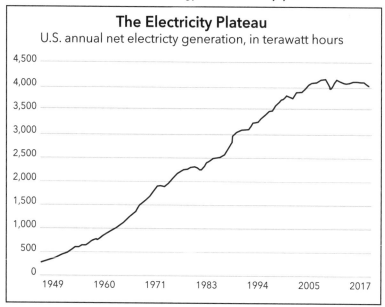

The Electricity Plateau
U.S. annual net electricty generation, in terawatt hours

Then suddenly, in 2007, the trend began to reverse. We used less electricity in 2008 and 2009. Now we're back to levels last seen in the 1990s. Expert research suggests several reasons for the unusual decline, including:

- Greater regulation.
- Rising prices.

- Better use of existing resources.
- Rooftop power from solar panels.
- A shift in our economy.

But now something is about to happen that's likely to change the trend. I believe electricity will be a hot commodity once more. This shift will make the stock prices of certain electricity companies skyrocket.

That big event revolves around electric vehicles. It's an important development that's at the intersection of two of the main mega trends that I track: the Internet of Things and new energy. The first electric and self-driving car — Tesla's Model 3 — came out in 2017. It was the first time the American public had seen a car that's everything many people — especially millennials — want in a car today.

They want their cars to be nonpolluting. They want to be able to talk on their phones or multitask safely while they travel. So, they want their cars to be self-driving. They want to be able to travel a longer distance without having to recharge. If that wasn't enough, they want the devices in their cars to connect to the internet.

The Tesla Model 3 provides all that and more. The compact four-door sedan seats five adults. It's designed to achieve a 5-star safety rating and has a range of 215 miles or more on a single charge. Its electric motor is smaller than one that uses gas or diesel. The engine is also capable of accelerating from zero to 60 in under six seconds.

Like all electric cars, the Model 3's interior is silent and vibration-free. Tesla's Autopilot feature lets the vehicle change lanes, read speed limit signs and brake if it detects a collision coming. It also features a large, TV-like touch screen on the dashboard that groups all the car's key functions into a single unit to limit distraction. And considering all these features, the Tesla Model 3 has a reasonable starting price of $35,000 before incentives.

The launch of the Tesla Model 3 signaled such a huge technological leap forward that a ton of people wanted in. In fact, the Model 3 got 400,000 preorders, worth upward of $10 billion total.

It was a moment when advanced technology took a quantum leap forward. As a matter of fact, I'm one of the people who preordered the Model 3. *And that's before the finished product was even launched.* As time goes on, millions of people around the globe will realize that the old fuel-guzzling mechanical car industry is on its way out.

How does an electric car beat driving a traditional gas automobile? Let me count the ways:

It's cheaper to run. The average American spends $1,627 to $4,000 each year to fill up their tank. Although electricity isn't free, it's a lot cheaper to charge an electric car. According to the U.S. Department of Energy, you can recharge an electric vehicle battery for as little as $2.64.

It has zero emissions. An electric engine doesn't emit toxic gases. It is 100% eco-friendly and contributes to a cleaner, healthier environment. It also runs quieter than a gas-fueled engine, reducing noise pollution.

It requires less maintenance. With an electric car, there is no need to lubricate the engine. Other costly engine work is unnecessary. You don't have to have the car serviced as often at all.

It's cost-effective. With tech advancements like the Model 3, the cost for maintaining electric vehicles has gone down.

It can save you a lot of money. Electric car owners report positive savings of up to tens of thousands of dollars per year. These vehicles can be fueled for very cheap prices. There are several government incentive programs that help you get back some of the cost of going green.

These are all contributing factors that add to the projected growth of the electric car industry, which is set to keep climbing higher. Just take a look at the chart below to see what I'm talking about. However, it's not just the rise of electric vehicles that will greatly increase the demand for electricity in the years ahead.

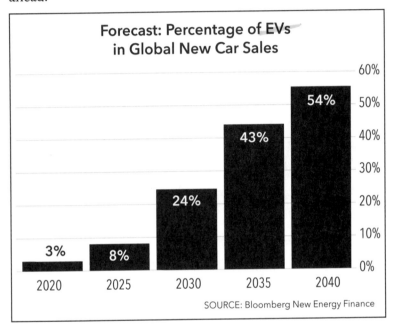

Electricity is one of the most important power sources in most industries. Its use makes up 38.1% of overall industrial energy usage. It's used in a wide range of processes such as automation, robotics and computer control. And these industries are growing by leaps and bounds. Now, it's true that industrial production dropped 20% during the 2008 recession. But now, U.S. manufacturers are moving into a more competitive position thanks to a stronger economy and less regulation.

As a result, manufacturing in the U.S. is expected to grow. It means greater industrial power demand for the future. Overall projections for world energy usage indicate an increase of 48% by 2040. There's just one small problem with this picture.

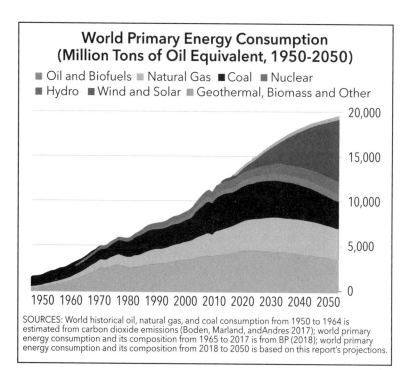

World Primary Energy Consumption
(Million Tons of Oil Equivalent, 1950-2050)

■ Oil and Biofuels ■ Natural Gas ■ Coal ■ Nuclear
■ Hydro ■ Wind and Solar ■ Geothermal, Biomass and Other

20,000

15,000

10,000

5,000

0

1950 1960 1970 1980 1990 2000 2010 2020 2030 2040 2050

SOURCES: World historical oil, natural gas, and coal consumption from 1950 to 1964 is estimated from carbon dioxide emissions (Boden, Marland, andAndres 2017); world primary energy consumption and its composition from 1965 to 2017 is from BP (2018); world primary energy consumption and its composition from 2018 to 2050 is based on this report's projections.

Our electrical grid is not ready for us to shift from fueling our cars with gasoline to filling them with electricity. Plus, there are the growing power demands of manufacturers. As I said earlier, between 2007 and 2016, our electricity generation capacity dropped by almost 2%. There are numerous reasons for the decline, but the biggest issue is regulation.

Research shows that it takes about five years from the submission of an electricity plan until the plant can begin construction. Every single thing about building an electrical plant is subject to permits, licenses and lawsuits. The bottom line is, catching up to 2007 in power production will take five to seven years. And it is estimated that going beyond that will take 10 to 15 years. But therein lies an opportunity. Between the coming demand for electric cars and the difficulty in supply, the companies that already produce clean energy are sitting on a jackpot. And at the top of the list is a company that has distinct advantages over its peers. It's creating a once-in-a-lifetime opportunity to grab massive gains.

Now, the important thing to keep in mind is that the next industrial revolution won't happen all at once. We're transitioning to an energy grid that needs to keep up with the demands of a growing society, a rising tech boom and a roaring economy. Remember, this is an electric revolution that's decades in the making. Just like Tesla reimagined how we can turn gas guzzlers into smarter, more powerful electric cars, one company will form the backbone of this transition to new energy.

And it'll start the electrification process at the source of innovation — in the factories, plants and facilities that design and create today's leading tech devices. If we can power our production lines with renewable energy, that move will have a quick ripple effect as new energy starts to spread from industry to consumers. From homeowners to small-business owners, the average Joe will soon have access to a power source that's not only cheaper to run, but cleaner and reusable.

Not to mention the cost savings it'll bring for local governments, which won't have to worry about supporting an aging power grid that could collapse at any moment. Understandably, early investors stand to make an impressive windfall by investing in this one company, as its new energy technology is set to impact every aspect of our lives in just a few short years.

One example I see that could profit from this energy revolution is First Solar Inc. (Nasdaq: FSLR). Based in Tempe, Arizona, First Solar designs, builds and sells solar-power modules and systems. And in the process, it's setting a new standard for how efficiently we can harness the sun's power.

But these aren't your ordinary solar panels. The secret to First Solar's high-powered success is the same technology that's inside every device connected to the Internet of Things (IoT): semiconductors. With a thin-film semi-

conductor layer, First Solar's sleek panels allow for electricity to be transferred and generated with higher yields and higher efficiency.

The film in the company's panels is so sleek, it's 33 times thinner than a single human hair. This ultra slim semiconductor technology is the key behind the quickening development of smartphones, wearable devices and computer systems — the heart of the IoT. And in these solar cells, it'll make up the heart of new energy.

What's more, First Solar is constantly researching ways to make its products reach higher yields. And the company's newest line of solar cells converts energy at 60% of the cost of its previous panels. In the field of new energy, efficiency is king. It's this efficiency that brings down the cost of running solar-powered systems, which spells savings on the user's end. Similarly, First Solar aims to compete with mainstream and legacy electricity sources — without the use of subsidies.

In the early days of solar energy, local and federal governments would give subsidies to those who made the switch to solar, since they eased the resource usage of the power grid. But at the time, converting a home to solar was a bit on the expensive side, and the support for solar just wasn't there.

That's precisely where First Solar comes into play, as its technology is winning over manufacturers and other businesses that look to reduce their energy costs while also limiting their waste. Then, once industrial companies have transitioned to new energy, we'll see a rush of less expensive solar options flood the consumer market as homeowners follow suit.

Right now, solar power is no longer limited by the enthusiast market. In fact, the global market for solar panels is set to reach $57.3 billion by 2022. That's great news for a company like First Solar that's set to spearhead the new energy transition.

For the moment, First Solar's target market is utility-scale project developers, whether they represent industrial businesses or government ventures. From there, it sells solar systems around the world, with 75% of sales currently based in the U.S.

But from my research, I believe that we'll soon see sales of First Solar's setups skyrocket worldwide, as the potential for harnessing solar power is truly global.

It's especially apparent when you consider that every hour, enough light hits Earth to completely power the world for a year.

It's as clear as day: To run an industrial, high-tech and rapidly developing world, solar is not just an energy option. It's a necessary part of a new energy "portfolio," along with wind power, geothermal energy, hydroelectricity and a number of other efficient sources. And since First Solar provides simple solutions to growing businesses and communities, it's paving the road for the future of new energy.

To solidify its place at the forefront of the new energy boom, First Solar has two business segments that offer different ways of making the transition to solar energy. First Solar's Modules division is responsible just for the design, manufacture and sales of solar units. From there, project developers can use the panels as they please. This branch makes up about 34% of the company's revenue.

However, First Solar also offers a more hands-on approach to solar conversions, and its Systems business segment is a perfect option for facilities that want the simplest solar transition — with all the benefits it entails.

As part of its comprehensive solar solutions, the Systems division handles the development, engineering, construction, maintenance and even some of the financing of enormous solar setups. This part of First Solar's business brings in just under 77.6% of its 2018 revenue.

As an added benefit, First Solar's power plant control system offers energy forecasting and scheduling capabilities. This adds reliability and stability to the company's projects, and it's all part of bringing smarter solutions at a cheaper cost. It's this attention to detail that allows First Solar to tackle enormous energy projects with ease.

One such project, the Mohammed bin Rashid Al Maktoum Solar Park, is a landmark turning point in the transition to new energy. Shown here, this one project covers an astounding 59 acres, and it uses over 152,000  individual solar modules from First Solar.

This one solar farm already produces enough energy to power over 600 households, and this clean energy would displace 15,000 tons of carbon dioxide annually. That's like taking 2,000 gas guzzlers off the road every year. In truth, a good chunk of First Solar's success is that solar power is a sustainable source of power. We don't have to mine it, and it's not going to run out.

First Solar's tech allows businesses to take advantage of a resource that's already available across the globe. Plus, the company uses cadmium and tellurium in its semiconductor technology. This is another crucial factor in First Solar's success, as it's a far cry from the archaic silicon-based panels that many solar companies have previously used.

Silicon is what makes up the majority of computer chips and other semiconductors that go into devices connected to the Internet of Things. And due to the heavy demands of the IoT, these devices are expected to consume all of the world's usable silicon by 2040. So, if First Solar had kept using silicon in its panels like many of its peers, it would only be a matter of time before First Solar's most critical resource ran out.

However, the company's management thought ahead and developed solar-panel technology that uses semiconductor material that will be available for decades. And in the process, this win-win strategy also made the panels more efficient and cost-effective.

At the same time, First Solar runs its business at high efficiency. The company recycles up to 90% of its leftover glass and semiconductor material. This eases the burden of disposal, and it also saves capital on material costs. This sets a standard for First Solar's operations, and when I dug into the company's financials, I saw a business set up for success across the board.

The stock itself will go up and down based on the price of photovoltaic cells, which are the parts of solar panels that convert light into pure electric voltage. PV producers were hit hard by the trade negotiations with China, as some solar companies were importing Chinese PV cells. As a result, the costs rose for some time.

But now, we've since cycled through the PV cell issue with China, and our economy is stronger than ever. Because of this, companies are willing to pay a bit more for solar PV cells. So, if you see slight volatility with the stock on its way up, this is an important dynamic to keep in mind.

Another factor that influences First Solar's business is its ties to the housing markets in one major way. It's only a matter of time until the company's large-scale solar solutions develop to the point where it's able to function at a utility scale. Put simply, we'd see First Solar's clever energy systems power entire neighborhoods running on efficient, cheap solar energy.

And as construction continues on new housing developments around the country, First Solar's tech will be in hot demand. Plus, I have reason to believe that the number of new communities on the market is about to explode...

See, there was a perception lingering in the market that a housing crash was right on the horizon, and this ended up hurting many housing stocks. However, I say that there was a "perception" of a collapse because, in truth, this effect was purely out of fear. People believe that the 2008 crash will happen again instead of looking at the facts.

More than anything else, we need a housing boom. And thankfully, that boom has just begun. Earlier, I told you about how First Solar has ties to two of our most profitable mega trends, which are the Internet of Things and new energy.

But right now, as this company develops its business and starts to grow dramatically, it's also affected by a new factor: the coming of age of the millennial generation. And as the quickest-growing generation in our country's history grows up, there's a sharp need for housing. This is where our stake in First Solar also becomes a millennial play — tripling its strength and profitability. But to understand just how this company fits into the housing cycle, we need to take a look at the state of our real estate.

In 2018, the average age of a house in the U.S. was about 37 years old. What's more, there were only 3 million units built between 2010 and 2016. That may seem like heaps of opportunity, but this 4% of the overall housing supply is nothing compared to the 92 million millennials on the hunt for homes.

In short, millennials are facing a twofold problem. We haven't been building enough houses for the past decade. And the current housing supply for sale is aging, desperately in need of repair and renovation. Now, it's crucial to keep in mind that millennials are more likely to use renewable energy, and that puts utility-scale companies like First Solar at the front of a roaring demand.

Remember, we're essentially buying into the stock at the bottom of both the solar energy cycle and the housing cycle. And when we buy at the bottom of both of these cycles, the only way to go is up. First Solar reflects all of these problems — the housing shortage, the need for renewable energy — and responds with a cost-efficient solution.

Now, First Solar has targeted its consumer base, giving millennial homebuyers and industrial facilities the ability to keep up with growing energy demands. At the same time, the company's financial side is showing that First Solar has the true momentum to power its future growth. And while the company took some time to find the right niche, its finances are strengthening.

In the early stages of its development, First Solar put millions of dollars from its budget into tech research. And it's because of that research investment that the company has the efficient technology that can power the communities of tomorrow. Now, First Solar's efficient tech is catching on with its market. Its rising revenue will form the bedrock that the company needs to keep growing.

From $1.3 billion on hand in 2016, to $2.3 billion in 2017, First Solar's cash on hand has skyrocketed. That ValueAbility is a crucial part of our GoingUpness system, and it secures First Solar's place at the forefront of the new energy transition.

Based on all my research, First Solar has the true momentum that makes it a rare profit opportunity. And this is what you want to keep in mind when vetting a stock. The kind of research I did for First Solar is the kind you'll need to spot the major-profit opportunities in our big mega trends.

PART
-5-

Hold Strong Hands for Success in the Stock Market

Every time another investor finds a reason to doubt me, I prove him or her wrong.

Every time.

My secret?

Strong hands.

You see, market makers want you to be weak.

They want the turbulence of this bullish market to force you to sell so that they can swoop in, take your stock and reap the benefits of your sales. It's a dirty game of manipulation that's been played in the stock market for decades.

My job is to get you to see the bigger picture. Stocks will go through periods of volatility. For me, I'm used to it being in the financial industry for more than 25 years. But for you, seeing a stock fall 15% to 20% is scary. It's a leap of faith for you to stay in these stocks. And I know it's hard.

However, to make the big money that we want to make, I have to tell you it will require guts, courage, conviction, belief and tenacity to fight through the tough times. This is how we'll get the big gains that I've been telling you about in this book.

The great thing about going through periods of volatility is that it flushes out weak hands. That leaves behind people who are willing to hold the stock. You're left with people in the stock market with strong hands. When buyers come in, the strong hands won't sell unless it's at our price. This is the moment where you ignore the pressure pushing you toward selling. This is where you develop a sense of faith that your stocks have those undeniable true momentum and GoingUpness qualities that, once the smoke clears, ultimately bring in the most gains.

It's the same with our mega trends. The important thing to remember is that their potential for growth is limited only by the potential of each mega trend to revolutionize our world and the economy.

Look, there are a lot of scary headlines out there. You see them on Yahoo! Finance. You see them on MarketWatch and CNBC. Nearly all the time, there are some number of people out there who think a stock market crash is imminent. Other people seem to think that there's going to be a financial crisis, or even a Great Depression.

I have to tell you straight up that I believe this is all pure doommongering. Ever since this bull market began in 2009 (and long before that) there has been someone to predict the absolute worst case scenario. I know because I've been in bull markets from day one, first as a professional money manager and then in my current role as a trusted guide to Main Street investors. Again and again, people have called for this bull market to end and, in truth, if you followed the doommongers, you got crushed.

Since 2009, the bull market has gone up threefold and more. If you bought into the doom argument and went to cash early on, you missed out. If you followed the folks who stayed in, you got rich. An amazing 878,000 Americans became millionaires in the last year. Yes, 878,000 Americans. And I can tell you that most of them did it through the stock market. I know because many of them are subscribers to my publications. They were able to buy incredible stocks like Foundation Medicine, NRG Energy and PayPal, and the most incredible thing about this is that it's all happened in less than two years.

I've gotten so many testimonials from people who have told us how they've made tens of thousands of dollars, some of them hundreds of thousands of dollars. In fact, we know that we have made people into millionaires as a result of the stocks that we've been telling them to buy.

The crazy thing about this bull market is that the so-called "smart money" have been completely and utterly wrong! You can see it from all the articles about failing hedge funds, for whom the sky always seems to be falling.

While these supposedly legendary hedge fund managers have told you that the markets are going to crash, the markets instead went up by 20%. In the same time period — just two years — my subscribers have made huge amounts of money. Meanwhile, the hedge funds have been delivering broken eggs to their clients for 10 years straight.

Look, the thing that really matters for stocks is earnings. Recent quarters have been among the best in stock market history. Companies benefited from the crash early on in the sense that things got so low that any kind of growth was going to be a high-percentage return.

That was not the case in the last few quarters, which started from a high level, and we still saw 25% earnings growth. That's just massive — absolutely huge. The stock market, in response, went down by something like 12% to 14%. Just think about that: Earnings for the S&P 500 companies grew by 25% in a single quarter and investors' reaction was to panic and sell.

Sooner or later, you're going to see people start to react normally to incredible earnings and bid prices up. I can tell you for certain that you are never going to get rich being in cash, and you're never going to get rich by selling too soon. And you're for sure never, ever going to get rich by following the wrong-way Larry's of the stock market, the so-called smart money, the hedge fund set.

Just remember: These guys are in it for themselves. They go out there to scare you after having bet on stocks to go down. As you panic, they and the other Wall Street insiders buy those stocks on the cheap from you, after you've dumped your shares. You once again find yourself on the outside looking in as stocks go higher, making even more people on Wall Street into multi-millionaires.

Everything that I'm looking at suggests that the insiders once again are gaming the system to get stocks from you on the cheap. You might see stocks starting to go up slowly at first. Then, suddenly, they will be at new highs and you'll miss out. This is why I say now is the moment to buy.

I am here to tell you what and why you should buy stocks associated with the great mega trends of our time: the Internet of Things, robotics and artificial intelligence, autonomous vehicles, blockchain, precision medicine, new energy and millennials.

Find the courage, find the conviction, find the belief to get in because I believe this market is setting up to go higher — and to go up by a lot. Find your strong hands. Many more millionaires will be minted, and one of them could easily be you.

APPENDIX

Make Explosive Gains in These 2 Markets for "Advanced" Investors

One of the great things about being an investor is that you have so many financial investments to choose from. If you're already investing, you probably have a comfort zone when it comes to trading. Maybe you prefer to simply buy and sell common shares of individual stocks. Or perhaps you'd rather invest in a mutual fund or ETF that tracks an index of multiple stocks.

But, as the saying goes, nothing ventured, nothing gained. By dismissing investments some may consider too "risky" or too "complicated" to understand, some investors are missing out on some of the most useful and potentially profitable investment vehicles available today.

As your knowledge of the market and your investing skills grow, you may want to explore other alternatives — particularly ones that could provide you with a greater source of wealth-building revenue. So let's get you started...

Market No. 1: IPOs — Don't Let Fear Stop You From Playing the Game

CRAZY … contrarian … nonconformist. You name it. I've been called every name in the book, and it's all because of how I invest.

That's because, where other investors are driven by fear, I'm driven by facts and what I know to be true. I never make shotgun decisions in any situation. Whether it's my personal or professional investing, I look at the raw data first. I always go by understanding of the facts and my experience of similar situations and trading setups.

Take, for example, the market sell-off of 2018. From October to December, every other headline on MarketWatch and Yahoo! Finance was predicting either a 2008-like recession or a market crash.

My colleagues and other professional investors feared the same. However, during arguably one of the toughest market sell-offs in history, I remained bullish that it was only temporary. And it was more than just my instinct and time on Wall Street that led me to believe this.

It was the hundreds of hours I spent scouring the data — researching the facts about companies, mega trends, the economy and the overall market — that fueled my positive outlook. By the first quarter of 2019, the market regained its momentum. And stocks were back up, reaching even higher highs than before.

Now, I know no matter which area of the market or type of investing you pursue, there's some level of fear. And it usually stems from the risks involved. When it comes to IPOs, fear is mainly fear of the unknown.

However, what I see in IPOs — and experienced firsthand — are their eye-opening profit potential. Yes, there are risks involved. But there are also rewards — I'm talking double, triple and even quadruple-digit rewards.

The table on the next page shows *exactly* how massive the profit opportunities are in IPO trading. Six months after eBay went public with its IPO, its price jumped from $0.31 to $8.13. That's 2,485%! This is all just a glimpse of the incredible gains that are ripe for the taking in the IPO market.

It pretty much goes without saying that the first thing you need to know before trading is what an IPO is. The industry definition of an initial public offering is the private-to-public transition of a company.

Issuer Ticker	Issuer Name	IPO Effective Date	IPO Effective Date Price	6-Month Date	6-Month Price	6-Month % Change
EBAY US	eBay Inc	9/23/1998	$0.31	3/22/1999	$8.13	2485.28%
FFIV US	F5 Networks Inc	6/3/1999	$5.00	11/30/1999	$56.56	1031.26%
JNPR US	Juniper Networks Inc	6/24/1999	$5.19	12/21/1999	$51.02	882.35%
STMP US	Stamps.com Inc	6/24/1999	$14.96	12/21/1999	$85.78	473.29%
ATRA US	Atara Biotherapeutics Inc	10/16/2014	$10.65	4/14/2015	$47.78	348.64%
GAIA US	Gaia Inc	10/28/1999	$4.82	4/25/2000	$15.18	215.00%
A US	Agilent Technologies Inc	11/17/1999	$18.82	5/15/2000	$55.32	193.96%
PHAS US	PhaseBio Pharmaceuticals Inc	10/18/2018	$5.00	4/16/2019	$14.50	190.00%
AKAM US	Akamai Technologies Inc	10/28/1999	$26.00	4/25/2000	$73.06	181.01%
AMZM US	Amazon.com Inc	5/14/1997	$1.50	11/10/1997	$4.21	180.53%
RCII US	Rent-A-Center Inc/TX	1/25/1995	$1.28	7/24/1995	$3.50	173.92%
ICHR US	Ichor Holdings Inc	12/9/2016	$9.77	6/7/2017	$26.24	168.58%
GORO US	Gold Resource Corp	9/14/2006	$0.90	3/13/2007	$2.40	167.27%
TITN US	Titan Machinery Inc	12/6/2007	$9.48	6/3/2008	$24.98	163.50%
LIVX US	LiveXLive Media Inc	12/22/2017	$4.00	6/20/2018	$10.43	160.75%
FSLR US	First Solar Inc	11/17/2006	$24.74	5/16/2007	$64.13	159.20%
EPAY US	Bottomline Technologies DE Inc	2/11/1999	$13.00	8/10/1999	$33.63	158.65%
AAOI US	Appied Optoelectronics Inc	9/26/2013	$9.96	3/25/2014	$25.43	155.32%
TREX US	Trex Co Inc	4/7/1999	$2.50	10/4/1999	$6.34	153.75%

Before an IPO, a company is privately owned. This means that its shares are not available for purchase on the New York Stock Exchange (NYSE), the Nasdaq or any other exchange at the open market. After an IPO, companies immediately become available for public trading.

I'll put it like this for scale: IPOs are to companies what Black Friday doorbuster deals are to retail stores.

Think about the flood of anxious buyers you see pour into stores like Walmart, Target and BestBuy on the news. All of those buyers are in search of a great deal for the highest value product. They're looking to buy that Samsung 60-inch LED flat-screen TV that's on sale for $375 and will surely shoot to three or four times that price the very next day.

Now take that scenario and flip it. Imagine those Black Friday shoppers are investors on the phone with their brokerage companies. They're anxiously awaiting the official announcement that a previously private-owned company with an amazing product is now available to be publicly traded at the open market. That's an IPO.

Private-owned companies go public for a number of reasons, such as to raise capital to reinvest and grow business, increase shareholder value, provide liquidity to investors and employees, and to use stock as currency for mergers and acquisitions. Here's a quick rundown of the different types of IPO investments:

Regular IPOs are when an investment bank sells shares to the public on the company's behalf.

Direct listings are IPOs where no bank is involved and a company directly lists its shares on the exchange. Spotify is an example of a direct listing.

Spinoffs are stocks of companies that "spun out" from a bigger company. For example, PayPal was spun out from eBay, which shares many characteristics of an IPO.

Exchange step-up occurs when a company moves from a junior exchange, like OTC or Vancouver, to a major exchange, such as the NYSE or Nasdaq.

However, from time to time, a company is able to get itself back to health and qualifies to get relisted on the NYSE and Nasdaq — which also shares similar characteristics of an IPO.

Timing is a critical factor in IPO investing. But there are a number of timing indicators to decide when to buy into an IPO. Placing an order before IPO — which can produce big gains fast — more often than not leaves money on the table. Getting in at just the right time often produces gains at least three times higher than buying at the IPO price. Every offering that comes public is a unique situation and will be traded accordingly.

If you've never traded IPOs before, you'll need to set up an account. To do so, you'll need to fill out a simple two-page form with your broker to get approval. Even if you've already traded stocks, make sure to get your brokerage account ready for IPO trading. Typically, this requires filling out a simple, one- to two-page form. However, this may vary by broker. To buy into an IPO, you call your broker and let them know you are interested in the IPO, and they will have you fund your account in cash for the number of shares you're interested in.

Market No. 2: Options — Navigate the Market Like a Wall Street Investor

Wall Street can be a difficult road to navigate — definitely for Main Street investors who are simply trying to grow their nest eggs without having to rely on high-priced analysts and their bevy of fees and complication lingo. It often means long hours of intense study to learn the tricks, vocabulary and calculations to get the inside knowledge and to truly leverage your dollar so that you're raking in some considerable profits.

And one of the most daunting tools at an investor's fingertips remains options. Just saying the word can produce a cold chill down the spine, but it doesn't have to be that way. In this section, I'll walk you through the basics of options so that you can not only learn the unique terms associated with these tools, but how you can make them work for you, earning returns greater than you might see by just trading stocks.

Introduction to Options

Before we jump headfirst into options, let's start with an analogy that will help ground options in your mind.

Let's say you and your partner have amassed a nice stockpile of cash, and you are house shopping. After doing your research, you've found the perfect three-bedroom, brick ranch home with a nice backyard and a two-car garage. The current owner is willing to sell the house for $200,000.

You agree that's a fair price for the home right now, but you're not ready to buy the house. Maybe you don't have the entire $200,000 right now or you'd rather use some of that money for other investments for the moment. Regardless, you offer the seller $200,000 for the house, but you will pay for it in three months.

The seller agrees, happy to wait three months to get the full price for the house. However, you can't just enter into a contract like this for nothing. No, to have the right to buy the house in three months for $200,000, you pay the seller $5,000. Not a bad deal. Now let's look at a couple possible outcomes.

Outcome No. 1

Two months pass from when you enter the deal with the seller, and it's discovered that George Washington, Benjamin Franklin and John Adams used to meet at this house on Friday nights to play poker. It's an enormous historical find! The house is now worth $2 million.

But the seller can't jack up the price or sell it to someone else because he is already contracted to sell it to you for $200,000. You purchase the house for $200,000 and then immediately sell it for $2 million, raking in a profit of $1,795,000 ($2 million minus $200,000, minus the original $5,000) — or 876% in just three months. Your partner and you are celebrating, ready to tackle your next investment.

Outcome No. 2

Two months pass from when you enter the deal with the seller, and it's discovered that the ghost of Blackbeard and his band of bloodthirsty pirates have risen from the grave. They have decided to haunt the house you're planning to buy. The value of the house has plummeted to $10,000 because no one wants to share a house with a bunch of pirate ghosts.

You close out the contract because you have no desire to purchase a house for $200,000 when it's worth only $10,000. The seller gets to keep the $5,000, which is your only loss on the investment rather than a loss of $190,000, or 95%, if you had purchased the house outright.

The same kind of opportunities can be found with options. They give you the power to leverage a smaller investment for large gains, while at the same time reducing your exposure to a single investment.

What Are Options?

Options are contracts. They represent an agreement between two people — the option buyer (holder) and the option seller (writer) — regarding a particular asset for a set period of time. The buyer of an option has the right, but not the obligation, to buy or sell 100 shares of a particular company or exchange-traded fund at a set price by a set period of time. The seller of an option has the obligation to buy or sell 100 shares of a particular company or ETF at a set price by a set period of time.

There are two types of contracts:

- **Calls:** A call contract gives the buyer the right to buy the underlying asset at a set price by a specific date. Calls are similar to having a long position in a stock. The investor's goal is to have the price of the underlying stock price rise sharply before the end of the time period so that his or her call contract becomes more valuable. One call contract gives you the right to buy 100 shares of the company at a set price (regardless of where it's trading in the market) by a set date.

- **Puts:** A put contract gives the buyer the right to sell the underlying asset at a set price by a specific date. Puts are similar to having a short position in a stock. The investor's goal is to have the price of the underlying stock price fall sharply before the end of the period so that his or her put contract becomes more valuable. One put contract gives you the right to sell 100 shares of a company at a set price (regardless of where it's trading in the market) by a set date.

When you're a buyer (holder):

CALLS = BULLISH

When you're a buyer (holder):

PUTS = BEARISH

Why Use Options?

You may be scratching your head, wondering why you would go through the trouble of using options when you can simply buy or short the shares of a company and rake in the same profits without having to learn this new vocabulary or additional steps. Options offer two great advantages that simply buying or shorting stocks can't deliver.

- **Leverage:** Leverage is almost a magic word among options traders. It represents the use of a financial instrument to increase the potential return of an investment. The best way to attack this concept is with an example.

You are looking to purchase 100 shares of XYZ Consulting, which is trading at $50, and you have a total portfolio of $20,000. It would cost you $5,000 ($50 times 100) to establish that position (not including any commission fees). You buy the shares, and now 25% of your portfolio is devoted to XYZ.

Your best friend, George, has the same size portfolio as you and decides to buy one call contract of XYZ that expires in May (let's assume that it's currently March). The call option has a strike price of $50 — in other words, he's willing to buy the shares of XYZ at $50 each. The call contract is trading at $2.50. He purchases it and pays $250 ($2.50 times 100 shares the contract represents). Less than 2% of George's portfolio is tied to XYZ.

There are benefits and risks related to both positions that I will get into later, but for now, I want to focus on leverage.

Let's say that two months pass, and the shares of XYZ rally to $65. You sell all 100 of your shares for $65 and rake in $6,500 — a gain of $1,500 ($6,500 minus $5,000), or 30%.

Meanwhile, George's call option is now worth $15 ($65 minus $50). He sells it for a gain of $12.50 ($15 minus $2.50), or 500%. Through the power of leverage, George was able to risk a smaller dollar amount — and a smaller portion of his overall portfolio — and lock in a bigger percentage gain.

It also works if you and George were wrong about XYZ. Let's assume that the company announces horrible earnings during the next two months, and the shares plummet to $30. You sell your shares for $30 and take a loss on the position of $2,000, or 40%. Your overall portfolio is now worth only $18,000, down 10%.

Now, since the shares of XYZ are trading below $50, George's call option is worthless (because no one wants to buy the shares of XYZ for $50 using the option when they can buy the shares in the market for $30). He suffers a 100% loss and is out $250. But even with a 100% loss on the option position, his entire portfolio is at $19,750, or down 1.25%.

Options give you the power to not only lock in some big gains without risking a huge chunk of your portfolio, but they also give you the opportunity to diversify your overall portfolio while limiting the impact of a single investment that goes against you.

• **Hedging:** As we all know, the market doesn't go straight up, no matter how much we wish it would.

Sometimes, we have to suffer a painful correction or two before a stock or even the entire market can get back on track to heading higher.

And the fear of a sharp pullback when you've got a portfolio full of stock positions can definitely keep you up at night. You've been invested in these companies for months, possibly even years, and you don't want to suffer a sharp 20% or even 50% pullback.

You're left with three choices:

1. Hold on to your stock position and watch the value plunge on bad news or just a general market correction. You're then forced to wait for the shares to climb back to their previous highs.

2. Sell your stock position so that you can sleep at night. Then you're forced to pay taxes on any profits you've made on that stock position. You also miss out on any potential upside if you're wrong about the pullback.

3. Hedge your position with a put option.

If you believe in the company and have a long-term outlook that is bullish, buying a put option as a hedge could help you weather some short-term losses and, at the very least, get some sleep at night.

A hedge is like buying a bit of insurance against a short-term disaster. And like insurance, you won't need it if disaster fails to strike; you're only out the premium you paid in that case. For some people, the cost of that hedge is enough to allow them to sleep soundly at night, knowing that their stock positions are protected against an adverse move in the market.

How Do Options Work?

There are five key components of an option:

1. **The Underlying Security** — All options are derivatives that have a large chunk of their value based on something else. Options can be traded on stocks, futures and indexes. Most beginning traders focus on trading options on either stocks or ETFs.

2. **Type of Option** — When it comes to options, you must choose whether to trade a call or a put. Call contracts gain in value as the underlying stock price rises. Put contracts gain in value as the underlying stock price falls.

3. **Expiration Date** — Unfortunately, an option contract can't last forever. There must be an expiration date. Options can be issued by the Chicago Board Options Exchange (CBOE) for as little time as one week or as long as two years.

4. **Strike Price** — The strike price represents the price at which you are willing to buy or sell the underlying security. This is not the price you pay for the option contract.

5. **Premium** — This is the price that you pay for the option contract, and it is calculated using the underlying security's price in relation to the strike price, time value and the expected volatility of the stock (but we'll look at this in more detail later). The price you see quoted with your broker or online will likely need to be multiplied by 100 because each option contract represents 100 shares of an underlying security.

Here's an example of a hypothetical options trade:

Let's say it is March 13, and Fake Tan Cabana is trading at $60. You are confident that the company's shares are going to skyrocket over the next six months, but you don't want to spend $6,000 to buy 100 shares of Fake Tan Cabana.

However, you can purchase one September 15, call contract with a strike price of $60 for $2.50. The premium (total cost) would be $250 ($2.50 times 100 shares per contract).

Now, as a holder of the call contract, you need the shares of Fake Tan Cabana to rally, but how much to get a profit?

First, you need to overcome the cost of the option. For a call option to gain in value, the shares of the underlying stock (in this case, Fake Tan Cabana) have to rally above $60.

To get your break-even price (the point where you start making a profit) add the strike price and the premium together. Breakeven: $60 plus $2.50 equals $62.50.

To make a profit on this call, the shares of Fake Tan Cabana need to trade above $62.50, or gain 4.2% from the price on March 13 of $60. The most you can lose when you purchase an option is the premium you paid. In the case of the Fake Tan Cabana trade, the most you can lose is $250.

Technically, your maximum gain is unlimited since there is no limit to how far a stock can rise. The only catch is that it has to happen before the option expires. In this example, let's say that you're correct. By early September, the shares of Fake Tan Cabana have rallied to $77 — a gain of 28%.

The September $60 call option is now worth $17 ($77 minus $60). Once you take into account the premium you paid for the option of $2.50, you're looking at a gain of 580% ($17 minus $2.50, divided by $2.50). But how do you collect that profit? With options, you have two choices when it comes time to start collecting your profits on a position.

Since each option on a stock or ETF represents 100 shares, you can exercise your option, changing it into actual shares. Using the example above, you could exercise your September $60 call for Fake Tan Cabana at any time after purchasing it. You would then pay $60 per share for 100 shares of the company for a total of $6,000, regardless of what the stock is trading for in the market. (This would be in addition to the $250 you paid for the option.)

From there, you could sell the shares at whatever the market price is and collect your profit, or you could continue to hold the shares of the company if you expect them to continue to rise.

Another avenue is to simply sell the option, closing out the position. That way, you capture the change in price of the underlying security as well as any time value still left in the price (don't worry, we'll get to time value soon), without ever needing to actually own the shares of the company.

Unless the option holder is looking to own the shares of the company, it's rare for a trader to exercise an option to capture any profits. The CBOE reports that roughly 10% of options are exercised, 60% are closed out and 30% expire worthless.

However, if your option has any value on the day it is set to expire, it is likely that your broker will exercise the option if you don't place an order to close out the position. (You will want to check with your broker to see how they handle it, as each is a little different.) But if you're long an option and it has any value at expiration, you will want to close it to claim that money rather than just tossing it aside.

The Option Premium

There are two main components of an option's premium — the intrinsic value and time.

- **Intrinsic Value:** The intrinsic value of an option is the difference between the underlying stock's price and the strike price. For a call option to have intrinsic value, the stock must be trading above the strike price. For a put option, the underlying stock's price must be below the strike price.

For example, Fake Tan Cabana is trading at $80. The September $75 call has an intrinsic value of $5. That's because if you owned the September $75 call, you could exercise the option and purchase the shares for $75 and then immediately sell them at the market for $80 — making $5 per share.

If Fake Tan Cabana is trading at $80, the September $90 put has an intrinsic value of $10. The intrinsic value of the option actually determined its "moneyness." If an option has some intrinsic value, the option is "in the money." If the strike price of an option and the stock price are approximately the same, it means that the option is "at the money."

If an option has zero intrinsic value and the strike and stock price don't match, then the option is described as being "out of the money." For example, Fake Tan Cabana is trading at $80. A September $90 call would be described as being out of the money. The shares of Fake Tan Cabana have to rally above $90 for the September $90 call to have intrinsic value.

- **Time:** The one concept that most new options traders struggle with is the time element of options. When it comes to trading stocks or ETFs, there's no limit to how long you can hold a position. When you purchase a stock or ETF, you need to be correct about one thing — the direction of the move.

When purchasing an option, you need to be correct about two factors — the direction of the move and when the move will happen. If you're wrong about one of those factors, there is a very good chance that you're going to suffer a loss on the position.

With options, their limited lifespan means that time is always ticking down, and that's a bad thing for an option holder. As the time shrinks on an option, it means that there is less opportunity for the underlying stock to move in the direction that you want. Let's look at an example of how time impacts an option's premium.

On March 13, Fake Tan Cabana is trading at $35.

The April 21 $35 call is trading at $0.85.

The October 20 $35 call is trading at $2.20.

In this example, the stock price and the strike price are $35. The option has zero intrinsic value. For our scenario, that means the remaining premium value is all time. Not surprisingly, the October call is significantly more expensive because the option buyer has roughly seven months of time for Intel to move. In contrast, the April call is less expensive because it has only one month.

- **Expiration:** All options have an expiration date, which comes in one of two forms — monthly and weekly options. Weekly options were introduced in 2005 by the CBOE as part of a pilot program and are now available for the most active stocks. They are usually available for each week through the next two months and expire on a Friday. Due to their short life span, weekly options will experience a faster rate of time decay (the rate at which the time value decreases from the option's total premium).

On the other hand, monthly options expire at the close of trading on the third Friday of each month. But not all months are available for trading at the same time. All stocks are put on an "option cycle." This is the pattern of months that options expire. The common cycles are:

JAJO — January, April, July, October

FMAN — February, May, August, November

MJSD — March, June, September, December

That means that at any one time there will be a minimum of three to four months of options available for trading (not including LEAPS, but we'll get to those shortly).

Luckily, you don't have to memorize a company's option cycle. You will be able to easily see which months are available for a stock's options by pulling up the options screen on places like Yahoo Finance or your brokerage. However, understanding that each stock conforms to a particular option cycle explains why you won't see every month available when you're looking to trade.

- **LEAPS:** Just in case you need a little more time for a trade to play out beyond a few months, there are also LEAPS. Long-Term Equity Anticipation Securities (LEAPS) are option contracts with expiration dates that are longer than one year. LEAPS are generally issued for the month of January and only two years into the future. Other than having a longer time until expiration, LEAPS behave the same as other options.

Placing an Option Order

Once you've done the research and you know which direction the security is going to head in, you know how far it's likely to go, and you know when the security is going to make its move. As a result, you've selected the best option to match your expectations.

You've just got to place the trade. Of course, options come with their own bit of language when it comes to actually placing the trade. When you are establishing a new long position (regardless of whether it is a call or a put), you will place a "buy to open" order.

For example, you believe that Fake Tan Cabana is going to rally over the next several months. So you may choose the June call contract to profit from that rally.

Your order: Buy to open the June 16 $45 call contract.

Now, let's say that time has passed, and you're sitting on a nice profit with the Fake Tan Cabana call. You want to close out your call contract and pocket the profit. You would choose a "sell to close" order.

Your order: Sell to Close the June 16 $45 call contract.

If you are looking to establish a short position with options (to be an option writer), you would "sell to open" a new short option contract. And to close out that short position, you would issue a "buy to close" order.

Now, you may be wondering … if a put contract gives me the right to sell the shares of the underlying company, do I have to own the shares before I purchase a put? No, you don't. You have the right but not the obligation to sell the shares of the underlying company. You can take profits on the put position without ever needing to trade the shares.

With all that said, it's time to start trading and maximizing your profits.

MORE FROM
PAUL MAMPILLY

Bold Profits
Premium Content

Paul Mampilly's®

Profits Unlimited

After turning his back on Wall Street, Paul started this flagship publication, giving Main Street Americans an opportunity to look over his shoulder as he uncovers truly unlimited profits — one triple-digit winner after another. His recommendations are based on his six-point GoingUpness investment criteria and the mega trends that have significant influence on the financial markets.

True Momentum

With this service, Paul implements the strategy he used to grow his personal account by 305% in just one year — 23 times more than the market. He's figured out how to identify 24 opportunities a year for capturing gains of 100% or more from pure, simple stock plays — in companies that have true momentum.

Rapid Profit Trader
with IAN DYER and PAUL MAMPILLY®

After years of studying other investors' behavior, Paul learned that it's very difficult to spot a good buy in the market. That's why he decided to develop a system that could take the emotional element out of investing. With this system, Paul has taken all of the guesswork out of knowing if — and when — a stock is going to make a huge breakout.

Extreme Fortunes

There are numerous investments primed to spin off huge windfalls that could put millions in your pocket. In fact, on average, 43 stocks rally 1,000% or higher every year! That means there are 43 opportunities every year — or three to four opportunities each month — to turn $1,000 into $10,000. With *Extreme Fortunes*, Paul aims to bring you the best of those each month.

The *$10 Million Portfolio* is Paul's asset-trading service that has no boundaries. Recommendations represent a slew of different types of asset classes, diving into analyses of domestic and foreign stocks, collateralized debt obligations, royalty trusts, warrants, crypto coins and more. By taking hold of opportunities in areas that Wall Street *isn't* looking into, Paul helps investors take advantage of diamonds in the rough.

After decades of investing, Paul learned that no stock ever goes up in a straight line. Even high-growth, high-potential stocks will face a bad week every now and then. Most buy-and-hold investors panic when their shares take an undeserved tumble during a "microcrash." But for Paul, it's a chance to grab phenomenal gains on stocks about to make a roaring comeback. That's why he teamed up with his internal analyst and co-editor, Ian Dyer, to develop a landmark strategy to riding rebound momentum.

📈 IPO Speculator
BY PAUL MAMPILLY©

Nine times out of 10, initial public offerings (IPOs) fall below their IPO price … leaving "insiders" holding the bag. Yet, over time, more than half of all IPOs go up 100% or more, and 10% go up 900% or more. If you can catch a new offering at what Paul calls its "Alpha Moment," the profits can be life-changing. Paul brings those Alpha Moment opportunities to you in *IPO Speculator*.

Paul Mampilly's®
Inner Circle

Inner Circle members are part of an elite group that can access all of Paul's investment research for life. Members also receive access to every new publication Paul releases, free of charge. Even better, members receive free access to one Total Wealth Symposium — and access to the conference livestream every year, in case they can't make the event in person.

**To get additional information about
any of these services, call toll-free**

1-866-584-4096

and speak to Paul's customer care team.

Or visit

https://paulmampillyguru.com
